EAST ORANGE
BY
CHRISTMAS

EAST ORANGE
BY
CHRISTMAS

My Father's Love Letters
from
London, 1933

JOHN L. KESSELL

SUNSTONE
PRESS

SANTA FE

Sunstone books may be purchased for educational, business, or sales promotional use.
For information please write: Special Markets Department, Sunstone Press,
P.O. Box 2321, Santa Fe, New Mexico 87504-2321.

Book and Cover design » Vicki Ahl
Body typeface » CG Times and Charlemagne
Printed on acid free paper

Library of Congress Cataloging-in-Publication Data

Kessell, John L.
  East Orange by Christmas : my father's love letters from London, 1933 / by John L. Kessell.
     p. cm.
  ISBN 978-0-86534-792-2 (hardcover : alk. paper) -- ISBN 978-0-86534-793-9 (softcover : alk. paper)
  1. Kessell, John Samuel, 1900-1963--Correspondence. 2. Lottridge, Dorothy, 1900-1963--Cor-
respondence. 3. Love-letters--United States. 4. Married people--United States--Biography.
5. Physicians--United States--Biography. I. Kessell, John Samuel, 1900-1963. II. Lottridge,
Dorothy, 1900-1963 III. Title.
  CT275.K458678K47 2010
  973.91092--dc22
  [B]
                                      2010044440

Published in

WWW.SUNSTONEPRESS.COM
SUNSTONE PRESS / POST OFFICE BOX 2321 / SANTA FE, NM 87504-2321 /USA
(505) 988-4418 / ORDERS ONLY (800) 243-5644 / FAX (505) 988-1025

To all those
who have experienced
or imaged
the love of a lifetime

John S. Kessell, MD and Dorothy Lottridge, MD

CONTENTS

1

ECHO FROM A SECRET PLACE

"Y ou know about the secret place," she said as she pasted the small round sticker marked $600 on my mother's mahogany secretary. She seemed bemused, our genial, antique-savvy friend. Well, I thought I did: "yes, those shallow little drawers inside the desk." "No, these." With that, she pulled open one of the small, seemingly solid columns flanking the tiny door of the central cubbyhole. It was hollow, less than an inch wide and perhaps five inches deep. There was something in it, evidently placed there long ago by my mother.

The letter was small in size, written on soft-blue note paper, folded once in the middle, and bearing the heading, "Burnham Lodge Hotel, Farnham Common, Bucks." I recognized immediately my father's hand. The date, August 24, 1933, registered as well. John Samuel Kessell, age 34, and Dorothy Lottridge, 33, had been married the day before in England. Tucked inside was a formal wedding announcement, printed sometime afterward, revealing the place, Wesley's Chapel, London, a fact I may never have known.

"Dear Mother and Father," the letter began. "Something so wonderful has happened to your Dorothy and to me," he wrote, revealing that John was addressing Dorothy's parents. The care he took with his readable but not especially elegant penmanship and the way the space between the lines increased over the three pages betrayed his excitement. "We are in love & so very happy."

They had met two and a half years earlier in New Jersey on a blind date neither had looked forward to. John, with his medical degree from the University of Adelaide in Australia, had booked passage in 1930 from Sydney to Victoria, British Columbia, taken the train across Canada, and from somewhere on the east coast apparently journeyed by coastal steamer to New York. He had contacts in America and hoped to get some practical hospital experience in urology, his specialty. Aboard ship, a pleasant couple, friends of Dorothy's subsequently identified as the Adriances, chatted with the eligible young Australian doctor and foresaw a match. Dr. Dorothy Lottridge, a graduate of Women's Medical College of Pennsylvania, had set up a private general practice on the first floor of her parents' home at 43 South Maple Avenue in East Orange, New Jersey, just across the river from New York City. Dorothy, too, was single.

But she was busy, and he wanted to see the sights of New York, not another hospital. Both, however, courteously agreed to their date and quite enjoyed each other's company. He met her parents; they may even have played bridge. "I quite liked her in the States," he recalled later, "but thought of her as a doctor." After some months, he sailed to the British Isles aboard the USS *American Banker* of the economical American Merchant Line, arriving in London on July 27, 1931, two days before his 33rd birthday. Traveling on to Scotland by train, he began almost at once an intensive course of study at the University of Edinburgh to earn a fellowship in the Royal College of Surgeons. He and Dorothy must have corresponded over the next two years, for when she took a vacation trip to London in the summer of 1933, she knew just where to find him. He, meantime, had gained his fellowship. (I remember well the "F.R.C.S. Ed." on his stationery, although he chuckled to us that he had to sit for the exam a second time.)

BURNHAM LODGE HOTEL,
FARNHAM COMMON,
BUCKS.

TEL. FARNHAM COMMON 275.

Aug 24th.

Dear Mother & Father.

Something so wonderful, has happened to your Dorothy & to me. We are in love & so very happy.

Do you mind having me for a son? I did like you both when I was in New York but it is a 'big' thing to have suddenly acquired you as parents.

Dorothy has told me something of your love & care for her & of what grand pals you all are. Please will you accept me into your little circle

The first page of John's letter, August 24, 1933

Writing from London on April 2, 1933, to a favorite cousin in Australia, 21-year-old Bettina Kessell (who gave me his letter 56 years later), he chided amiably,

Betty, me thinks you misjudge me. Because I do write at length about skating, golf & outings of one kind or another you seem to imagine nothing else enters my existence . . . . Believe me, young lady, the things I write voluble about are the 'high spots' in an existence that was until recently overfilled with studying.

Yet he had managed to see, while still in Edinburgh on March 18, the scrappy international rugby match between Scotland and England, a defensive battle won 3-0 by the Scots. "Yesterday I saw part of the boat race. Unfortunately the incoming tide drove me from a carefully selected vantage point. Still it was interesting." Into the envelope, he had tucked a memento from America, a thin brownish strip on which he wrote, "This is birch bark. It makes good writing material. It was birch bark the Indians made canoes from."

Even with fellowship in hand, John's medical future looked uncertain. The worsening global economy in the years after the Great War was stifling people's hopes. He had secured a low-paying job in London, in essence a residency at "St. Paul's Hospital for Diseases (Including Cancer) of the Genito-Urinary Organs and Skin," Endell Street, Holborn. He expected to stay on about nine months. The fellowship, he hoped, might allow him to retain his specialty in urology, but he had his doubts. "In time of depression," he mused in a note to Bettina's father, "such select beings are apt to be overlooked & may even go hungry." He thought he might have to become a general practitioner. "Still, having spent so much time & money on my specialty, I will stay in it if possible." He resolved to keep alert to all possibilities.

Cousin Bettina Kessell (courtesy Penelope Denyer)

Amid the pulsing eight million human souls of greater London, from the artful street urchins to the Duchess of Kent, provincials from every corner of the British Empire clustered in pockets of their fellows from Fiji, India, Canada, or South Africa who had come on pilgrimage or to study, find work, or carouse. Fresh arrivals almost always knew some friend or family member who had preceded them.

The Australian community was particularly tight. John had plenty of contacts, among them an Australian nurse by the name of Gwennie Oats. He and Gwennie had enjoyed time together on staff at the Broken Hill Hospital in the silver-mining outback of far western New South Wales. Just a fortnight after his marriage to Dorothy, Gwennie would ring him up from Cornwall.

Studies had kept him in Edinburgh the better part of two years. Now, by George, he would get to know London, explaining to Bettina that he was in the very heart of the city, living in the hospital complex. "True, the neighborhood is not salubrious & the quarters are cramped & somewhat grimy, yet one cannot have everything." John especially lamented his paltry salary "with theatres around each corner, the opera house in the next street, strange restaurants aplenty & a London season about to commence." But by no means, he lectured his young cousin, did he aspire to become a social butterfly. He would, however, "see a few of the events, Wimbledon, Henley, the Derby, the Royal Tournament & such like."

John loved tennis best. And the Wimbledon championships of 1933, held at the All England Lawn Tennis Club between June 26 and July 8, proved memorable in the extreme. On the women's side, the heavily favored Helen Wills Moody of the United States, dubbed by the British press "Miss Poker Face," had won five of the six previous Wimbledon titles, never losing a set. This time, facing Britain's Dorothy Round before a delirious crowd, she finally dropped a set, but still won the match 6-4, 6-8, 6-3.

Another American, Ellsworth "Elly" Vines, Jr., a veritable cornstalk at 6' 2" and 143 pounds, had won the 1932 championship, blasting Briton Bunny Austin off the court with a stunning 30 aces in only 12 service games. In 1933 Elly would face the unruffled, 25-year-old, hugely popular "Gentleman Jack" Crawford of Australia. Whether Crawford's countryman Dr. Kessell secured a ticket to the final, heard it on the wireless, or read about it in the papers, my dad cheered. Crawford, losing the first set 4-6, saved break point after break point in the second to prevail 11-9. The players traded the third and fourth sets, 6-2, 2-6. Then, unhurried, "Gentleman Jack" closed out the championship match, 6-4.

The most reported event of that summer was the World Economic Conference held in the cavernous gray and green reception hall of London's Geological Museum from June 12 until July 27. In his act of welcome, rigid, handsomely uniformed, 68-year-old King George V looked out over a nationalistically attired sea of nearly a thousand delegates seated at long desks and representing 66 countries arranged alphabetically in French. Their agenda—weighed down by staggering war debts, currency manipulation, vast unemployment, and trade barriers—was thrown off course from the start by the news from the United States. Recently inaugurated President Franklin Delano Roosevelt appeared intent on going it alone, creating a unilateral planned economy. Failing to find common ground on anything but fear of the future, representatives to the London conference simply dispersed. The next domino fell in Geneva later that year when Germany walked out of the World Disarmament Conference. Rearmament put people back to work.

Meanwhile, on Monday, August 7, 1933, Dr. Dorothy Lottridge from America arrived in London on the USS *American Farmer* (sister ship to the *American Banker*), unexpectedly alone. A prior invoice saved in a scrapbook showed round-trip passage for her and another woman, together totaling $343, outbound from New York on July 28. As destiny would have it, Dorothy's best friend and traveling companion Helen Goodell (whom my sister and I knew later as Aunt Helen) broke her leg and could not make the trip.

John knew Dorothy's schedule. Although he failed to greet her at the foot of the gangplank, as he wanted to, he later proved a companionable guide. They saw the Russian ballet and attended services in Westminster Abbey. She met his friends. Then, on a trip together "to a cathedral town," he discovered "the girl underneath." Two mature professionals, they fell in love with childlike glee. He had always wanted, he confessed to Bettina in another letter, "to 'go off the deep end' and to have nothing else matter save 'her.'" He proposed and she accepted. With less than a week of her vacation left, they threw themselves into plans for an immediate wedding: "a special license, a visit to the American Consulate to learn the welcome news that Dorothy would have a dual nationality, & then an irate minister to soothe."

With the date set for two days hence, her lovestruck Australian husband-to-be posted a letter to "Dr. D. Lottridge, Dartmouth House, 37 Charles Street off Berkeley Square." He could scarcely contain himself. He had found his "darling behind the Doctor." Then, taking a phrase from the Irish poet Bartholomew Dowling without acknowledgment, he added, "What a high & haughty person is that Doctor, quite all right for other people but I have no ills for the Doctor to cure but I have lots of longings for you, dear one, to satisfy." A life together, home, children, a medical practice, all seemed unbelievably and wonderfully at hand. "Thank God," he exclaimed, "for cathedral cities, for matron's sitting rooms & for London towns." On Wednesday, August 23, "we were married," he told Bettina, "very quietly in Wesley's Chapel, City Rd. Strangely enough, the four of us at the altar were doctors."

That same day, a hurricane surged up the east coast of the United States forcing a monstrous tidal bore in the Potomac River, drenching Washington, D.C., with more than six inches of rain, and causing widespread flooding that swept a train off its tracks. Eighteen people perished in the storm. In London that day, BBC technicians at Broadcast House put on the world's first televised boxing match, an exhibition between British middleweights Archie Sexton and Laurie Raiteri. John and Dorothy took no notice.

After an excellent lunch at the Waldorf, "what it consisted of I know not," the newlyweds repaired 24 miles to Burnham Lodge Hotel, a lovely former country estate on the borders of famed Burnham Beeches. There were few guests, the weather shone gloriously, and they vowed to continue a tradition of honeymoons no matter how brief. Thursday evening, after each had written to their new in-laws, they retired to be alone together for a few more short hours.

The following day, Friday, they lunched again in London, and that evening after he slipped her a final love note, Dorothy sailed for home on the *American Merchant*, carrying her new husband's letter written on that idyllic Thursday to her unsuspecting parents in New Jersey. His exuberant lines just over a week later to Cousin Bettina supplied the details of their hasty nuptials. Swelling with pride, he even suggested that she write to his new wife, which she did.

They had put no postage stamp on the hotel envelope. She would hand his profession of love and caring to her parents in person. "I did like you both when I was in New York," he had written,

> but it is a "big" thing to have suddenly acquired you as parents. Dorothy has told me something of your love & care for her & of what grand pals you all are. Please will you accept me into your little circle. . . . At the moment I have merely myself, my love & my good name to give Dorothy, but I feel so confident that I can make good & Dorothy happy that I have no fears for the future.

She was an only child, he one of four, two boys and two girls. He hoped her father and mother would approve of "our apparent precipitate action." The main purpose of his life would be to make their daughter happy. "Please accept me on trust as a son. Yours affectionately, John."

In New York harbor, with the gangway lowered, Dorothy's parents came aboard the *American Merchant* on Monday, September 4. Before she could present them with either the news or the letter, an awkward moment occurred. She was paged as Mrs. John Kessell: "Radiogram for Mrs. Kessell." It read simply, "ALLS WELL DARLING LOVE JOHN." In relating the incident, she never told us exactly how it played out. In London, meantime, her exultant husband was assuring Bettina that "the separation is hard, but just think of the future ahead of us." Dorothy "is no ordinary girl—I can hear Uncle say, 'They never are.'" Marriage had changed his whole life. "It has given me a purpose. No longer do I wish to travel alone. I want to set up a home & then have a family. Twins to start with. How does that sound?"

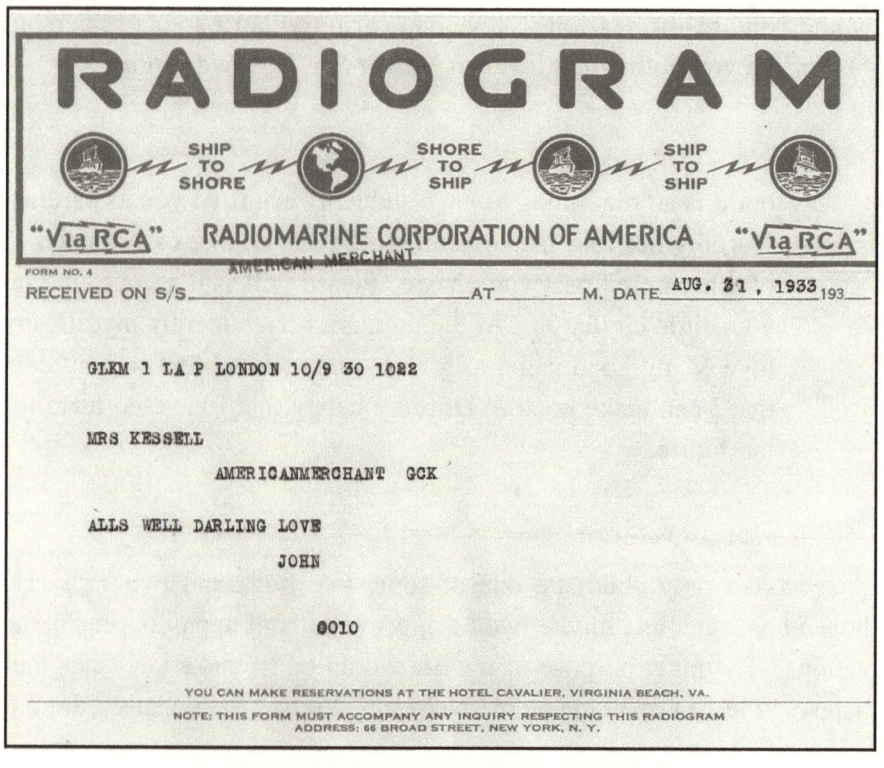

John's radiogram, August 31, 1933

During the last few days of August, all of September and October, and most of November 1933, the Atlantic Ocean separated them. John, a romantic if ever there was, wrote to Dorothy every day, morning and night—not infrequently at 1:00 or 2:00 a.m.—placing in a single envelope four or five letters at a time. Each little envelope (4 1/4" x 5 1/4") he addressed proudly to "Mrs. John S. Kessell, 43 South Maple Av., East Orange, New Jersey, U.S.A.," pasting in the upper right-hand corner the appropriate George V three-halfpence stamp. And she saved them all.

In weaving together these excerpts, I have treated the letters as historical documents, nowhere altering my father's wording and only correcting silently a rare misspelling or inserting a comma, hyphen, or question mark. Regrettably, my mother's responses, which he so cherished on receipt, have gone missing. She saved his every letter in a speckled cardboard 4" x 5" file box. After my parents' death, I transported that file box from place to place, remembering only that it contained some sort of documents relating to them or perhaps to my grandparents. Not until decades later, with the discovery of the especially treasured letter kept in the secret place of my mother's desk— his eager reintroduction to her parents—did I finally open the small file box and read for the first time my father's tenderhearted love letters from London.

2

A "PRECIPITATE" COURTSHIP, WEDDING, AND HONEYMOON

Dead tired but still awake at 1:30 a.m., John recalled his bride's departure. He had waited at the dock for a lift "& so saw the boat go out. I was glad you were in your cabin & not on the deck." Dropped off at London Bridge, he had walked back to the hospital.

But, Darling, that is not what I wanted to say to you. Oh how I do love you. I really could not go off to sleep without just telling you how much I do miss you. But, Darling, I am so sleepy. How I wish you could be in my arms. Wasn't it all so very wonderful?

So weak he could hardly hold the pen, promising to write more in the morning, he conceded sheepishly, "We really did not have much sleep last night."

John awoke on Saturday, August 26, profoundly lonely yet joyful. "Letter writing is apt to make so many of the tender caressing things I want to say to you rather absurd." But he knew Dorothy would understand. Memories of Thursday, the day after their wedding, came crowding in. "It was early morning. The daylight was only a flickering glow when through the window I saw a strange cone-shaped fir tree set in a lawn." Hauntingly beautiful, the scene held his attention only fleetingly, for "lying asleep on the other bed was a lovely woman." He next conjured a proper Victorian intruder to whom he addressed himself.

Ah, you ask, "What is this you, base bachelor, are up to?" Ha! Ha!, I laugh as I snap my fingers in your face. "Your fears are most groundless. Bachelor!, did you say? Why it is applied to a race of men I have no time for. Sir, that lovely woman is my Wife & what is more, don't you ever forget the fact!" Oh, it is ludicrous to see him retire out of countenance & discomfitted.

Her new and lawfully wedded husband had then, with impish clear conscience, awakened her with a kiss and held her tight. "It was beyond description, such contentment, trust & understanding."

Pen in hand, John did not miss a morning or night between August 25 and November 21. "I do like coming back into my little pokey room after my bath & sitting up in bed & greeting you before I dress. I set out on my day's work in the right mood." While inventing many ways in his letters to express his love for her, his frustration at their separation, and his hopes for their future together, John revealed much about himself, his daily routine, and how he coped in London without her. Gradually, a stroke at a time, recalling certain days and happenings, he painted a fuller picture of their courtship, from which one fact seems clear. My mother had seduced my father.

Burnham Lodge Hotel

Burnham Lodge Hotel bedroom

The vacation of Dr. Lottridge in London had not begun as Dr. Kessell intended. Remembering in early November, he put his chagrin in the form of a fairy tale:

Once upon a time not so very long ago a very beautiful Princess with brown impish eyes, dark hair, a rosebud mouth & cherry lips made to kiss & be kissed & skirted by elusive but very expressive dimples . . . decided she would go on a far journey to see the wonders of the lands across the sea of which she had heard so much. She took ship in a large vessel & after divers & sundry adventures with strange men she arrived in the land of chalk white cliffs & strange contrasts. Alas & alack she did know but a few people in that land & on her arrival they were not waiting to greet her.

On her own, Dorothy had conveyed herself to the elegant Dartmouth House in the heart of Mayfair.

Soon along came a runner bearing a note from an apologetic friend telling a tale of an unsympathetic train service that considered not the desire of people who wish to be present to meet Princesses. Shortly afterwards followed this friend himself, a very ordinary man. With him the Princess fared forth to see some of the wonders of this strange city. Darling, the above is but the beginning of a rather amazing romance.

John did not reveal how much time had elapsed—hours, days?—before this very ordinary man called upon the princess, or how the princess had fared during her first ten days in London. Neither, unfortunately, did either of them keep a diary. Counting back eight weeks from the start of their separation, however, on Saturday, October 14, John wrote: "We have a name of our own for each day of the week: Oxford-day, Westminster Abbey-day, Matron's room eve or decision day, Wedding Eve day, Wedding or Canterbury Day, Burnham Day & Auf Wiedersehen Day or Boat day." Thus he filled in their calendar from Saturday, August 19, through Friday, August 25.

Socially, they had begun at least a day earlier, the previous Friday, when they attended the Russian Ballet with his friend Aubrey Lewis, likely one of the four doctors at the altar. That enchanted evening wafted back to him three weeks later. He and Dorothy seem also to have shared time together on a visit to Canterbury the Wednesday before, "our doings at Canterbury."

The real whirl began on "Oxford-day," Saturday, August 19. "That was a very wonderful garden where we sat & were together." Evidently, back at St. Paul's Hospital that evening, they had sent his colleague Lewis Davies off to bed "& had our momentous talk. How full my head was. I have never tried to face up to so many stark facts at any time in my life before. As I left you, I made my memorable confession: 'I like you but you have no attraction for me.'"

Over and over in his letters, he chided himself for that ill-considered remark. "Two weeks ago, no three weeks ago, tonight you made me eat my words. What a little devil you were. Gollee how I wanted you then & how I loved you for making me want you." Elsewhere he had to admit, "it was not long before I was eating those selfsame words & was so hungry for the one to whom they were addressed." "Yes," he confessed yet again, "after due deliberation, I have come to the conclusion that maybe I do like you, but of course, Oh! No! You have no attraction for me!!! Quite!!! You little devil to throw that up at me. But I love you for teasing me. How I do love you."

That memorable Saturday night, John had slept very little, awakening Sunday morning "with one or two large questions to answer." Greeting her five Sundays later across the waters, "Good Morning, Fair One, Are we to go to church this day?" he remembered that they "dined at Dartmouth House & then went along to the Abbey." Her townhouse hotel, a 16th-century mansion sumptuously refurbished in the 1890s by Lord Revelstoke, cannot have failed to impress the American lady doctor.

Sunday afternoon the 20th found them listening to the speakers in Hyde Park. Walking leisurely on, they crossed the Serpentine. "I stopped to pay my respects to Peter Pan," John wrote to her four weeks after that, "& told him you sent your love & that we had agreed to tell our children all about him & his adventures." They had sat in Kensington Gardens watching the people and their dogs. "If only you were in a chair beside me & I had your hand in mine," he mused on the same spot, "I would be very, very happy." He would have much to make up to her. He had been to the fine Victoria and Albert Museum, where "there are fronts of old English houses, period rooms, furniture, clocks, jewelry, porcelains & Japanese colour prints." How he wished he could have run off with several of the latter for their future home.

What happened in the hospital matron's sitting room Monday night overshadowed all else on an eventful day. They had already begun exploring the possibility of marriage, "just in case 'You did attract me.'" After lunch with Davies that day, John and Dorothy settled on going first to check with the American Consulate, then back to the registry office, and on to see his friend Norah Marsh. "Finally in matron's sitting room I came out of my Rip Van Winkle sleep & beheld in front of me My Princess, & most wonderful of all she agreed to share my throne with me. And I am the luckiest of men."

Though he teased her playfully in his letters, he obviously relished the seduction. "Law! But wasn't that a grand night in that sitting room." Another time, "How you tantalized me, you adorable minx. Matron's sitting room was a great place." And again, "It is scarcely fair to me you being so very, very adorable & huggable & kissable, but of course 'You have no sex appeal for me.' Just let us repair to the matron's sitting room. Quite!"

On another Monday night, remembering their honeymoon, John blamed her gladly for his great longing.

D 1585 No 18

CERTIFIED COPY of an

Pursuant to the Marriage

Registration District   Fin

1933.   Marriage Solemnized at ____ Wesley's Cha

in the District of ____ Finsbury

No.	When Married.	Name and Surname.	Age.	Condition.	Rank
51	August Twenty-third 1933	John Samuel Kessell	34 years	Bachelor	m.E Ade F.R. Edi
		Dorothy Lottridge	33 years	Spinster	M.D me Col Phi

Married in the ____ Wesley's Chapel. ____ according to the Rite

This Marriage was solemnized between us, { John Samuel Kessell / Dorothy Lottridge }   in the Presence of us, { Lewi / Floren / aub

I, ____ George H. Wheal ____, Authorised Person under th

Register Book of Marriages of the above-named Building.

WITNESS MY HAND this 20th day of October , 1

If you did not have brown eyes from out of which looks such a provocative devil, ones that lure me—a mere man—on & promise so much, then you have such lips—Darling, how I love to kiss them & long to do so—bordered by the most exasperating of dimples that I would catch but cannot, try as I might. . . . And you, most adorable of women, are my wife. Darling, I am yours most completely & utterly. What have you done to me to bewitch me so? Whatever it be, never undo the spell for it means so much to me in every way.

ENTRY OF MARRIAGE.

M. Cert. (25)
A.P

Acts, 1836 to 1898.

Insert in this Margin any Notes which appear in the original entry.

City Road

in the County of London

6	7	8
Residence at the time of Marriage.	Father's Name and Surname.	Rank or Profession of Father.
St. Pauls Hospital Endell Street	Stephen Kessall	Methodist Minister
37 Charles Street Berkeley Square	Silas A. Lottridge	Chemist

monies of the _Methodist_ by _Licence_

and in the Presence of { William Osborn Barratt

Authorised Person for the said Chapel

Act, 1898, do hereby certify that this is a true copy of the Entry No. 57 , in the

Authorised Person.

Copy of John and Dorothy's Marriage Certificate

Tuesday, the day before the wedding, had begun badly. There were too many things to do: church, ring, flowers. Right off, John received "my shock from the minister," unexplained in the letter since she knew what he was referring to. Next he had to dash out and be measured for a new suit, call at the bank, return, and be fitted. At the registry office, he was "informed that it must be at Wesley's Chapel or nowhere if we were to be married next day. I was very down in the mouth when I met you at the Piccadilly. What a catechism I was put through ere things straightened out." Whatever his problem with the clergy, John later referred comfortably to "our dear old minister," Methodist Rev. William Osborn Barratt, who signed their marriage certificate just shy of his 72nd birthday. The younger Rev. George M. McNeal subsequently wrote to the groom's father Stephen in Australia, also a Methodist minister, expressing the honor of having married the two doctors and describing Mrs. McNeal's favorable impression of the bride.

What a place to have been married, the groom thought back eight weeks later. Although rather boxy and severe on the outside, "It is a very famous church & the graveyard associated with it & near it contains the bodies of many illustrious people including John Wesley, Susan Wesley, John Bunyan & Daniel Defoe." When the American Consulate required a copy of "the lines" as evidence they were legally wed, the Rev. McNeal was happy to provide it. On their wedding day, Dr. Davies later told John "that Dorothy was so very excited in the cab & that she shook like a leaf at the altar."

Reliving their wedding in a different letter, he knew it was

only the beginning of our great adventure. Darling, it is grand to be alive. How lucky am I to know that such a girl as yourself cares for me, loves me & wants me &, Darling, to know that we belong to each other, are each incomplete & lack an essential part for complete expression of the best that is in us when we are not together is a wonderful & inspiring thought.

After lunching on whatever delicacies the Waldorf set before them, they took the Premier B Coach out to Burnham Lodge Hotel, arriving late in the afternoon of the 23rd. Looking back on their hasty wedding, John thought,

How very wise & right were we to become man & wife eight weeks ago. As well as anticipation of the wonderful times ahead, we have the memories of a perfect realization of a consummation that was beyond my wildest expectation. I reached happiness & contentment undreamed of & vouchsafed to few men. How wonderful you were in every way.

Each Thursday until they were together again, John recreated their Burnham day, "our perfect day," the one full day of their abridged honeymoon. As he awakened on September 28, his mind drifted back five weeks.

What memories. A blissful contented day. The sun shone & all around was beauty. To get lost in the Forest, to have a little hut to rest in & in which to hold you close to me. Darling, truly we have made an auspicious start. Another few such days to start off our life together ere we face things together. Truly God is kind.

During their honeymoon, short though it was, they had began composing a lovers' code. "Enthusiastic" or "active cooperation" became their term for sexual intercourse, the opposite of "wild acquiescence." She must have laughed at his use of the word "quite." "Darling, how I do love you. If you say 'Quite' to me like that, I'll turn you up & spank you. How does that appeal to you. It will be good exercise for me, you say."

"Darling, do you have your backache cure handy?," he wrote slyly on another occasion without supplying a description.

How I do look forward to it. Do you remember our Thursday morning three weeks ago? Everything was beautiful. There was such bliss & contentment just being with you. The breakfast in the little alcove. The walk in the forest, our game of putting. My! but I will need to practice to keep my end up. Our dalliance upstairs, our quiet talk sitting in the game [room], tea outside under the trees, our evening walk in the forest. Darling, it is all so vivid & so very beautiful. How I do adore & love you, my very own wife.

Finally, each had written to the other's parents "& retired to be alone together."

On a subsequent Thursday night, John asked her, "Darling, do you ever feel awed & a little frightened of such happiness as is ours? It is so overwhelming. There is nothing I would not attempt for you." He looked forward to being a loving father. "Darling, it is a wonderful thought to think upon you [as] the mother of my children. Fortunate children indeed. My pen lags tonight for I am thinking so many exquisite thoughts of you, my love, of us & of ours-to-be. Goodnight, wonderful wife of mine."

Whatever the circumstances, getting up to close the window in their Burnham room Thursday night became a joke between them. "One more hug & a big kiss & I must really shut the window." On a wet, foggy October morning, pondering their schedule when finally they would live together under the same roof, he offered the following: "The only solution I can find is for me to wake up considerably earlier . . . else I will not manage to get that window shut in time to dress." "After mature consideration," he wrote in another letter,

I have come to the conclusion that I am afflicted, that it is chronic by now—from intensity not from the known duration—& quite incurable but that it needs constant attention such as can be given by only one physician I know of. She recently changed her name & is now called Mrs. John Kessell. Into her hands I place this case unreservedly. You are a darling to take charge so willingly. But as I remarked on another occasion, while I talk to you 'the window stays open.'

He may have surprised himself a bit one morning when, in a passionate mood "half awake & half a-dreaming," he visualized

a dark-haired girl with a creamy just faintly olive skin, with brown eyes, a nose that is just right, white teeth that are puppy sharp, a mouth that I love so, it is small, the lips are soft & delicious & bordered by elusive dimples all set in soft-skinned cheeks & chin. She has such a desirable body. . . . Oh, Darling, I do so love you from the crown of your head to the tips of your toes.

Never did he forget the rapture of Friday morning after the wedding. Awakening before she did, he looked out upon "a beautiful view through the window, big trees in a lovely garden & all shrouded in the intriguing mystery of morning mist with its ever-changing fantastic shapes." It failed to hold his gaze, for Dorothy was smiling in her slumber. She looked so peaceful. Desire overcame him, and "I did kiss her as she waked & then crept in beside her & held her to me till we two became but one." He sensed, thinking back on that morning, what a force the two of them would be together. "We really will do things worthwhile & because we know such limitless happiness we will aspire to make others whole & happy."

Back in London that afternoon, August 25, a few friends evidently joined the newlyweds for a luncheon, among them a genial Australian, Mr. Thompson, who just a few days later got knocked over by a motor car, more a fright than a serious injury. John had accompanied his new wife to Southampton, boarding the *American Merchant*, helping her locate her cabin, and befriending the stewardess, whom he implored to take good care of her.

"Yes, Darling," he professed a month later, "we will always be sweethearts & lovers & we will have many, many honeymoons, on the slight pretext or even without any we will run all by ourselves & live again Burnham Lodge Hotel." Then, from the perspective of ten weeks, he distilled their courtship and original honeymoon in these words:

> Darling, to ascend to such sublime heights alone would have been an unforgettable experience, but to do so together brings us closer & more attune than could years of ordinary companionship. We must have our up & down, our differences & disagreements and our fits of temper & upset but if we can remember our visits to the mountaintops & how incomplete they would be without the other it will help us to forget & forgive.

You have married no saint, in fact a very ordinary man, but he does love you so.

She satisfied him perfectly in every way, "intellectually, spiritually, & physically."

3

ST. PAUL'S HOSPITAL
AND COLLEAGUE DAVIES

A teaching hospital devoted to urology, St. Paul's dated from the late 1890s. First located in a house in Red Lion Square, where it served as a largely outpatient facility treating venereal diseases, it was moved during the 1920s to Endell Street, where Lewis Davies and John Kessell lived, treated patients, and performed surgery in 1933. The place ran on a low budget. The two of them seem to have been the resident doctors, with a Mr. W. K. Irwin as supervisor. The unquestioned star of the staff was Horace Powell Winsbury White, whose book *Stone in the Urinary Tract*, published in London in 1929, was followed by his thousand-page *Textbook of Genito-urinary Surgery*, appearing in Edinburgh and Baltimore in 1948.

What relation young Lewis Davies might have been to O. Picton Davies, Esq., Deputy Chairman of the hospital board, John never revealed, but like the other Davies, Lewis was a Welshman from Cardiff. The gracious young Davies stood as a witness, if not as best man, at John and Dorothy's wedding. Only two days after Dorothy sailed, however, bachelor Davies found himself in big trouble that "developed like a bolt from the blue. He said I might tell you," John reported.

For five or six years, Davies had "knocked about with a girl from near his home town. He wrote her love letters as a man will." Eighteen months before John related this story, however, Davies had told the girl he wished to break off their engagement. She agreed reluctantly, insisting that she still loved him. He had been honest with Betty, his current lady friend, and with Betty's father about his previous affair. Then, suddenly, the other girl and her mother showed up in London, demanding that Dr. Davies marry her. When he refused, the girl's mother demanded £3,000 or else she would file a breach of promise suit. She knew that the last thing the young doctor wanted was a court case. Even though she reduced her claim to £1,500, Davies would consult a lawyer. Sympathizing with his colleague—"I will do everything I can for him"—John added uncharacteristically, "Aren't the people swine."

Monday morning, August 28, another hot day, he had a time getting "poor old Davies" out of bed. But John was thinking all the while of Dorothy crossing the Atlantic. "Have you found any interesting people on board? I feel sure our friend the stewardess is looking after you most carefully. She was a dear the evening you sailed." In London, Dorothy had met a number of his close friends, including two young women, Lil and Stella. John admitted to his new wife his surprise at Lil's reaction to their marriage. "The one, Lil Walsh, has felt it more than I ever would have imagined but she is ungrudging in her congratulations. Stella is thrilled through & through." Returning to the theme two days later, he added,

It was quite interesting yesterday to note Lil Walsh's reaction. She did wish us well but was quite affected by the fact that I was married. She told me that she would have been deeply hurt if I had married the Australian girl for we would not have been suited & the girl was so obviously after me. With you it is different. She is sure I am very lucky indeed & she is just judging from appearances. Little does she know how very fortunate I am.

One day when Lil and Stella came to lunch at the hospital, they brought "a fine Chinese jar on a stand" as a wedding gift. "You will be delighted," John wrote, asking that Dorothy drop them a note. A few days later, he saw the two of them off by train to catch their boat back to Australia. Lil, once home, wrote to John's parents, assuring them that he had married "the right one." As for the scheming and unsuited Australian girl, we can only speculate that Lil Walsh had in mind John's nurse friend, Gwennie Oats.

John himself soon referred to Gwennie without mentioning her name to Dorothy. "Another girl friend of mine—an Australian girl—rang me up from Cornwall to congratulate me. She was delighted I had married an American. She was genuine in her pleasure at our happiness. Aren't people very decent."

Given the concentration of the family name Oats in Cornwall, it is likely that Nurse Gwennie was living with English relatives. John's people were also from Cornwall. His grandfather and namesake, an engine man in the tin mines, had married Elizabeth Chenalls at Illogen in 1860. That John Kessell's enforced emigration to Australia had occurred in 1872. The most plausible family story is that Grandfather John, a married man, had got a village lass pregnant and been told in no uncertain terms to take his lawful wife and four children and find himself a new home. Another story makes the Kessells "free traders" (smugglers) across the English channel, akin to the pirates of Penzance. Either way, my paternal grandfather had grown up in Australia to become a circuit-riding Methodist minister.

But it was Lewis Davies's problem with women that concerned John late that August of 1933. Handing the R.M.O. (Resident Medical Officer) designation over to Kessell, Davies spent a few miserable days, then reached an agreement to pay £1,000 in yearly installments of £100 to the jilted girl and her mother, thus keeping the matter out of court. Kessell, meanwhile, covered in the wards and clinic. He performed a hernia operation for Davies. It went well, which pleased him for it had been two and half years since he had done one at Bayonne Hospital in New Jersey.

Although shaken by recent events, Davies now packed his trunk and headed off for his turn in Edinburgh. "I hope he is successful but I think he will be very fortunate if he does manage it first try." Meanwhile, a genial young doctor named Kennedy, "a real good sort & extremely popular with everyone," took Davies' place at St. Paul's. The hospital was bustling. "This evening," wrote John, "I have been busy trying to fit five patients into three beds." Then he was up in the night attending to "one of my Hebrew patients." Two nights later, he admitted an emergency patient another hospital had refused.

He was never reluctant to discuss his cases with Dorothy. After an unhurried round in the ward one Sunday, he had seen "a V.D. patient who has developed an hysterical paralysis" and had given him "some galvanic stimulation." Then he changed some dressings and took a history. "Darling, I do marvel at the change in myself & thank you accordingly. I am so much more purposeful & confident." In a subsequent letter, he was even more emphatic:

Oh Mother-of-my-children-to-be, you can never fully know what your coming into my life has meant to me & to those I come in contact with & have to work for & with. I have so much greater understanding & a very definite desire to do good & so to justify your faith in me.

Personnel matters also came Dr. Kessell's way. A couple of days after joining two orderlies in a game of darts that convinced him he needed "lots of practice," he was listening to complaints about a bossy new "sister," or head nurse, "very efficient but too officious" and "as tactless as can be." Foreseeing trouble, he would "endeavor to straighten things out & have the ward working smoothly. I started lectures to nurses again today." The next day, "I talked to both the new sister & orderlies & told them what I expected & that it was up to them to work together."

Observing surgeon Winsbury White in the hospital's operating theater, John concluded that he was "rather spectacular." Hence, when Winsbury White's secretary rang asking him if he would assist at an operation, John was elated. "I get paid & besides I consider it an honor to be asked." The surgery turned out to be at Beaumont House, "one of London's 'swish' nursing homes."

"Darling, I must be extra good at my work." In contrast to his experience with Winsbury White, it had fallen to Kessell to assist "while some atrociously bad work—I refuse to call it surgery—was done by one of my chiefs." The tragedy was that the man did not know how bad he was. "He started by cutting a V out of the internal meatus then he tried to remove some fibrous prostate by enucleation & finally had a hole in the rectum. He has left me to look after the patient." Appalled, John swore to Dorothy, "Ever we will treat our patients as human beings & not simply as cases."

Busy as he was, Dr. Kessell kept a close eye on the calendar. The *American Merchant* should have docked in New York on Monday, September 4. Dorothy sent a cablegram immediately, which reached him the next morning. He was overjoyed that she had arrived safely "& that your father & mother approved of our action (and isn't that American? Quite! You say.)"

Yet he could hardly wait for her letters. He wanted to learn from her, "Do you like me writing in such a lover-like way?" A woman friend to whom he confided his whirlwind marriage found the story romantic and "rather the sort of thing I would do. This surprised me for I regard myself as rather prosaic." Now, as he counted the hours in anticipation of her first letter, the entire hospital took an interest. "Young Olive," who awaited every mail delivery and reported the results, "is quite sure the ships are being delayed by storms. Brewster, the night porter, is very sympathetic for he used to have to wait for his letters when he was in India."

It was Brewster's job to awaken the doctors each morning, which on occasion he forgot to do. Reporting somewhat later, John explained to Dorothy that Brewster "is a real Cockney alright. He has been yarning in my room with Kennedy & me since he brought some tea up. I do wish you could be here & listen to him. He is most amusing. 'It ain't 'arf.' 'I did that an all.' 'Gawd Blime.' He is the genuine article." Friend Aubrey Lewis also offered advice. "When I told him how I haunt the doorstep waiting the so-far-barren postman, he quietly reminded me of the laws of transport whereby it takes time for an object to be carried from one spot to another."

At last they arrived, her first letters, fittingly on Thursday (their day), September 14. When Aubrey was late for sukiyaki that evening, he reread them and "was able to be alone with you. Your letters brought you very close to me, Darling." Happy and relieved, but "too late for a show," he and Aubrey went to the movies and saw *I Was a Spy*, the war story of a Belgian girl who had reluctantly engaged in espionage for the Allies, starring the beautiful Madeleine Carroll. "I liked the Mickey Mouse better," John confessed.

Dorothy must have written nearly as often as he did. "You are so grand you let me say all sorts of things, some sensible, lots nonsensical, yet you pretend that it is all important to you. How I love you for it." Her repeated admission that she longed for him as lustily as he for her comforted him. "You said that wanting me was more acute than [you] had believed it would be. Darling, in my case longing for you is a deep-seated ache situated in my chest." One Thursday night, reliving their time at the Burnham Lodge Hotel, John began his letter,

I have an almost irresistible desire for you tonight. If it was possible I would be with you. Your presence would calm me. My love for you is so tremendous a force that I feel it in every part of my being. At the moment my longing for you is far greater & something different from mere physical desire. I cannot express myself but I think you will understand for I have read such a similar feeling in your letters.

Yet he could make light of their constant correspondence, as he did on the last day of October.

Do you think old man Atlantic is of a curious turn of mind & listens in to all the thoughts sent winging their way across his vast domain? If so methinks I can hear him say, "Those two doctors again. They are never silent, one or the other & often enough both sending thought messages. It is always the same old theme. Still I should not grumble. I remember how I felt when Venus was in these parts." Then he would sigh for the good old days. Darling, how fortunate are we to have our own good days ahead. Oh, No, I would not change [you] for any Venus.

Lewis Davies, meanwhile, had written from Edinburgh, "telling me he became scared & pulled out at the last moment." He should at least have sat for the exam, John allowed, but "I know the feeling & can sympathize." Betty was worried about Davies. Having gone "missing" for several days, when finally he showed up at the hospital, he regretted not having given the exam a go. "He is rather chastened in spirit, poor blighter. Darling, I am so pleased to have it behind me." That fact encouraged him when he thought ahead about the state and national board exams awaiting him in the United States.

Despite further treatments, his hysterical paralysis case did not improve. John had been avidly reading *Fear*. "It is an amazing book & one from which I will gain much." The author, John Rathbone Oliver, respected psychiatrist and Episcopal clergyman, had studied under Sigmund Freud and taught currently at Johns Hopkins University School of Medicine. John wanted to talk to Dorothy about the book,

for it contains so much of interest to us as medicos and to our patients. How very little I know about psychological medicine has been brought home to me by my patient with hysterical paralysis. I do not know how to set about treating him save physically. It is very humbling to have to admit that one cannot adequately treat a patient.

From *Fear* John copied out for Dorothy a quotation from Thomas à Kempis:

It talks about time, love & is descriptive of my love for you & of my experience & feeling: "Nothing is better than love, nothing higher, nothing wider; because love is born of God & cannot rest except in Him. Love feels no burden, pleads no excuse of impossibility but attempts what is above its strength, for it thinks all things possible. Though weary, love is not tired; though alarmed, it is not terrified. He that loveth is free & not bound."

After receiving her photographs, he felt so much closer to her and made it a habit to "talk" to her regularly.

It is raining outside & dark. I have drawn the atrocious red curtains, set the table light at my elbow, placed cigarettes on a chair beside me, changed my shoes for slippers & my white coat for my woolly dressing gown, lighted the gas fire & seated myself in a big armchair. Best of all you are looking at me so interestedly from off my table. You are not smiling "our playtime smile" but you are saying in your look "Yes, I would like you to talk sensibly to me for a while. I am interested to hear your ideas of *Fear*."

Well then, first, John thought the author's religious views tended to overshadow the psychological thesis so well set out early on. The afflicted patient must of necessity gain a faith and have implicit trust in his or her doctors. While reading the book, he thought he might want to apply practical psychology himself. "On reflection I have decided I must work in conjunction with a competent psychiatrist." He also decided that *Fear* would make a fine Christmas present for his father in Australia.

St. Paul's renowned Winsbury White had attracted an international following. "Winsbury White operated this afternoon," John reported in early October. "His perineal operation is very neat indeed. Eisenrath, an eminent urologist of many years standing in Chicago but now of Paris, was looking on." A couple of days later, Kessell was "amused" to run into Dr. Lonsley of New York, associate professor of urology at Cornell University, whom he had seen operate at New York Hospital. The American was sure he recognized John. "By the time we had reached the operating theatre we were getting along famously. Mr. Irwin [John's supervisor] asked him if he remembered me from New York. Lonsley replied glibly, 'Oh yes. We are old buddies.'" When Dr. Kessell explained that he was coming to the United States to join his new wife, also a physician, Dr. Lonsley insisted that they look him up. Such a promising contact.

In the same letter, John mentioned a case Mr. Irwin had given him. "Instead of doing a radical hydrocele I decided to do an orchidectomy. I am interested to find my confidence a permanent thing. Darling, how I do look forward to running a service of my own. I am sure it will be well run." Although he knew they would experience rough roads at times, he predicted that "We will run well in harness together. . . . Won't it be grand saying 'May I introduce my wife' or 'This is my husband. Have you met him?' How proud I will be."

When Lonsley returned to St. Paul's to observe Winsbury White perform his special perineal prostatectomy, he greeted Kessell "as an old friend, 'And how is the pride of Australia this morning,' he said. Of course Winsbury White was impressed." Praising the operation, Lonsley

instructed Winsbury, "You teach this young fellow your operation & then when he comes across to New York I will give him a clinic to do it in." He added, "But you must let him do some cases." Winsbury promised to do so. It is a chance that may turn out trumps. As Dr. Lonsley left he said, "Make my place your headquarters in New York." Of course I do not build on such remarks yet they form an excellent introduction.

Always conscious of the exams that would be required of him in America, Kessell tried to keep abreast. The hospital's nonresident cardiologist kindly offered help.

Today I went across to the Royal Free Hospital & listened to some hearts. I heard systolic & presystolic & diastolic murmurs. I wondered which was which. I could tell if there was a murmur or not, but that was about all. Medicine, it is a large subject. Still it is a start I have made.

A few days later, he fretted, "What a lot I have forgotten. I bought a book on medicine to read & refresh my knowledge." He was tenacious. On another day, "I attended a heart clinic—Oh! No! not for attention to my heart. Surely, doctor, you have not forgotten that you have my heart in your safe keeping."

His days at the hospital remained full but varied. "I have had a busy day," he reported at the end of September,

& have been exceedingly well washed. I had my usual morning bath. This afternoon I went for a grand swim. It always does me a world of good. This evening I decided to wash away the smells of a postmortem that I took about two & a half hours to do. It was vastly interesting for from a primary carcinoma of the penis secondaries were scattered all over the body especially in the lungs & liver. There were none in the bones.

At times, he recommended to her what had worked for him. "Yesterday morning I did a very neat suprapubic cystostomy under evipan. I had fifteen minutes of good anaesthesia. For small jobs it is splendid."

On another occasion, he performed the same procedure, but the patient proved less hardy. "He seemed quite alright for some hours & then he developed respiratory failure & died. I did not think him a very poor operative risk. The actual cause of death I do not know. I suppose it must have been uraemia." A week later, he boasted of their remarkable success at St. Paul's Hospital with radium therapy.

> In a case of carcinoma of the prostate we left radium in the gland after a perineal exposure for 14 days & removed it today. From being a stony hard gland it has become firm & fibrous to the feel. It is astounding. Probably the man has secondaries but if we relieve him from any urinary symptoms it will be worthwhile.

Davies, meantime, plagued by his uncertainties, proved a frustrating colleague. All of a sudden, he decided that he and Betty should get married right away and that Kessell should be his best man. He wanted a ceremony just like John and Dorothy's, same church and all, rather than a big wedding in Cardiff. "Davies & I began talking of his future, whether he is to get a practice & give up his idea of a consultant job or whether he is to put off marriage for 2 yrs. & get his extra degrees. We talked at length." John urged his friend to consider seriously the second alternative.

The next night, after attending a show together, the two young doctors talked even longer.

Davies is a very interesting man to study. We saw Josephine Baker, the famous negro or half-caste dancer. Among other things she did her celebrated banana dance. It was one of the most sensual exotic dances I have seen yet Davies saw nothing sensual in it. I talked to him about the importance of love play in sex life. He sees no need for such thrills. How very much he & Betty may miss. Darling, how much we have to be thankful for I am realizing more & more. Being mature, tolerant, & understanding gives us such an advantage as we start off.

Josephine Baker's banana dance

By the end of October, Davies had given up all pretense of studying. He seemed to have abandoned the idea of returning to Edinburgh, although he would not admit it. At times, he slept until two or three in the afternoon. "I would not mind doing all the work if he was studying but as it is it is annoying." More galling, Davies had made time to give an anesthetic for a private doctor, for which he received payment over and above his hospital salary. "He has found a gold mine in someone outside who gets him to do jobs for him. I have no such luck," John lamented. Davies promised to cover one evening, but did not show up until after midnight. "His unreliability will get him into trouble in practice. At times I like the chap. He certainly was good to us."

Yet rumors that Davies had arranged a partnership and was going to marry Betty the next Saturday had the hospital staff in turmoil. "There is no doubt about this place being something of a madhouse & causing those living here to act precipitately." Davies was out. He evidently planned for Kennedy to replace him. The day before, Kennedy had received approval to replace Kessell, but that very evening he walked in with a letter offering him a position as ship's surgeon aboard a Blue Funnel boat leaving for Australia in mid-December. Recently engaged, Kennedy thought that if he could bring a wife, he would accept. "It looks very much as though this place may have new men before the end of the year for come what may I leave in time to be with you by Christmastime."

Finally, Davies told Kessell, "in about two words," that he had resigned and was off to Cardiff, evidently to join a private practice there. Instead of marrying Betty straightaway, he had bought a new car. He might show up again briefly at St. Paul's. "But for casualness & lack of consideration for others I have not met his equal. It will be lots better next week having Kennedy here definitely." And that was the last John reported to Dorothy about his memorable colleague Lewis Davies.

3

ENTERTAINMENT

Despite his scant salary, heavy demands as a doctor, and further study, John went out frequently to dinner or to see a show. Yet curiously, in London where international cuisine beckoned on every corner, he mentioned in his letters to Dorothy none besides Japanese. He loved fixing sukiyaki at the table, always commenting on his guests' skill with chopsticks. (Later in life he favored spicy Indian curry with chutney and relished candied ginger.)

Almost every week, John managed to see a stage play or movie, despite at one point lamenting, "Darling, isn't it strange how I have lost my desire to go to shows & entertainments? If you were here to go with me it would be different." Ten days later, however, he related to her that "the hospital has done well in complimentary tickets of late." That evening, he and a good friend from Edinburgh had attended "'After Dark,' a revue. It was patchy, part good, part poor. Darling, we will go every now & again to New York to see some shows & not settle into complacent indifference to what is happening on the stage, won't we?"

On Saturday, the day after Dorothy had sailed, John consoled himself on a bus trip through the lovely English countryside—"Rolling grassy parks, spreading trees & hedges. You know it so well"—to the Swan Hotel in Petworth, West Sussex. Lil Walsh, Stella, and "Auntie" (otherwise unidentified) went too. "My love for you is so great that it almost makes me afraid," he wrote to Dorothy on hotel stationery. He had so much to tell her.

> I am a strange mixture of happiness & sorrow. Happy at the wondrous thing that has happened to me & you know my sadness but it won't be for long. These girls have been such dears to me. They have let me talk & talk about you & about our doings. Of course the most wonderful things I have not wanted to talk to them about. They have kept me from thinking too much about our separation.

But think he did. He counted on Dorothy to excuse his "inarticulateness. I know you do. If only you were here in flesh—you are in spirit—I would use actions not words. Gollee! how I love you. Did you say 'Gone off the deep end.' And how!"

Petworth House, one of Lord Leconfield's country estates, he reckoned, ranked with Windsor Palace and Hampton Court, with its "huge Georgian house & most beautiful grounds. . . . How I wish we could have wandered about as I did with the girls." The day was grand, only marred by Dorothy's absence.

> I really felt that to appreciate to the full the beauty of all I saw I needed you present. It was an actual feeling of some part of me

missing. I would exclaim in wonder at something outstandingly beautiful & the girls would add "This would be perfect if only." They understood & were dears.

Back in London, he described for her the marvels of the place, a classic English country estate set in a park overpopulated with fallow deer.

Lord Leconfield has the finest and largest collection of pictures in England, the carvings, the sculptures, furniture & tapestries are priceless. He keeps two full packs of hounds & a pack of beagles. The kennels are lots cleaner than many houses. How you would have loved the hounds, especially some puppies. He has cut his stables down to about thirty instead of fifty. There is an indoor riding school. He has a 'real' tennis court the floor of which cost £15,000 & he keeps a professional. There are ordinary tennis courts, a sunken garden, flower gardens & a most wonderful park with lots & lots of deer.

It had done him a world of good to be away from the hospital.

His rounds and studying took up so much time. "At the moment," he wrote in early September, "although I do love going out with friends I am loathe to give up the time. I am most certainly going to make this job a worthwhile one for me." Still, he managed. One evening, after sukiyaki with Lil, Stella, and Auntie, they saw *Proscenium*, by famed London playwright Ivor Novello, which had opened at the Globe earlier that year. Novello himself took the lead opposite Fay Compton.

It was most interesting & dealt with the stage & the love of a man & woman who each had a stage career & of the way they adjusted themselves. Despite their ups & downs they had an abiding love for each other that won out. Darling, I saw such a parallel to ourselves with marked differences. I had a much greater understanding of the play because of our experiences than I could ever have had otherwise.

John also critiqued the latest motion pictures for Dorothy. He and their friend Mr. Thompson, "a fine gentleman," shared an evening. "We saw the film 'Cavalcade.' It is certainly well worth seeing. In fact it is one of the finest films I have seen." His opinion of *The Cuckoo in the Nest* stood in sharp contrast. "It was an example of an excellent comedy ruined as a film." Such plays, he thought, could not be made into successful movies. "If this film goes to the U.S.A. & is shown as an English talkie then it will give a poor impression of them."

So focused was John on his absent American wife that he rarely mentioned current affairs. Yet when he learned that a young woman he knew had just returned from six months working in a German laboratory,

I rang her & she came around & we spent the evening yarning. It was most interesting to talk with someone who has lived in Germany. The German people only learn what is considered good for them of events in other countries or even in their own land. As a people they are intensely national & militarism is born in them. Apparently Hitler has done something for Germany in saving it from Communism.

The year, after all, was 1933. Adolf Hitler had emerged in January as German chancellor. By spring, a National Socialist (Nazi) dictatorship was firmly in place and the blatant persecution of Jews had begun. In protest, Albert Einstein renounced his German citizenship, sought passage to the United States for himself and his wife, and quietly took up residence in New Jersey at Princeton's Institute for Advanced Study. Three weeks after John wrote the above paragraph to Dorothy, Germany abandoned the international disarmament talks and announced its withdrawal from the League of Nations.

Although he "liked the simple creed of the nonconformist church" Dorothy had mailed to him, John attended Wesley's Chapel sporadically. During an evening "choral harvest thanksgiving service," he let his mind wander. Had there been no church, no ceremony, he confided in Dorothy,

we would be married in the true sense of the word. Such a tremendous thing as our love is not bound by any puny man-made service. That happens to be a visible contract for the sake of the community. We are fortunate that the way was clear for that extra. Loving you so completely there was nothing else for me save to devote my life to you, or if that were not possible when the realization did come to me, pass through blank despair the outcome of which no one could foretell. But, Darling, we are part one of the other each incomplete without the other. "I have given my love my heart, and I have my loves." How much more force & vitality flows through me from my new heart. I realized the necessity for such alterations but knew not where to apply until in Matron's sitting room you showed me.

One Saturday evening, John pined, "How I wish we were going together to Westminster tomorrow. Still it will soon be Riverside Drive

Church." He preferred Westminster Abbey to St. Paul's Cathedral. Attending an evensong at the latter, he compared it unfavorably to the Abbey. "The minister's voice echoed through the lofty domes. One does not feel the same atmosphere there." Writing three years later to John's cousin Bettina, Dorothy commented,

> I was greatly interested in your remarks about St. Paul's. All my life I had wanted to see it and for some reason I couldn't explain I wasn't a bit impressed by it. Isn't London the most fascinating city in which to explore? John and I had such a thrilling time there. We are so anxious to have a vacation in England but I'm afraid it will be years before we do. Love, Dorothy.

Apparently she had met John's friends Horace and Eleanor Humphreys, whose home in Blackheath allowed him an occasional pleasant escape from his hospital routine. "As usual," he wrote to Dorothy after one such visit, "I thought of how grand it will be to have our own home & sit by the fire & just yarn or read or do whatsoever the spirit moves us to do." (Although I do not remember my dad later in life ever using the verb "to yarn," he delighted in reminiscing and storytelling.)

One Sunday after services at Wesley's, "our church," he took a boat down the Thames "under the various bridges, past the Tower & other historic spots & through the 'Pool of London' & by many of the large docks" to Greenwich, a city rich in historical associations. Drake, he told her, had sailed from there in his *Golden Hind*. Nelson studied at the Naval College and his body lay in state there. William and Mary landed at Greenwich, and General Wolfe lived and left from there. Walking across to Blackheath, John enjoyed Sunday tea and an evening of "yarning" and listening to the wireless with Horace and Eleanor.

The Humphreys were a couple John and Dorothy could emulate as they entered into their new life together.

It will be just grand. Ours will be a life of moods, sometimes we will be jolly as school kids, & romp about, at times grave as judges & discuss serious subjects, anon we will be romantic & tell fairy stories, again we will be reformers & seek ways & means of helping others, or we will be doctors & discuss the latest in medicine & surgery, ofttimes we will be parents & talk of our children but ever we will be lovers, incomplete the one without the other, happy in each other's company & prepared each to give & to take.

Another friend, Dr. Atkins of the Park Prewett Mental Hospital northwest of Basingstoke, invited John for what turned out to be a most refreshing weekend in late October. After dinner at St. Paul's and *The Fare Includes Romance*, "a light but very enjoyable comedy," they ate supper and caught a 1:00 a.m. train. They did not arrive at their destination until 2:30, after half an hour's drive from the station in Atkins's car.

Even after another late, late supper and yarning with his friend, John found time in the wee hours to write to his wife. He had not realized how fed up he was with his scanty quarters at St. Paul's until he saw how Atkins lived at Park Prewett. "To walk up a wide staircase to the floor that belongs to the medical officers & consists of large, spacious, well-furnished sitting rooms, one each, large bedrooms, a splendid billiard room & a large dining room. Can you wonder that I am reveling in it?"

He "lazed about" on Saturday. "I played snooker quite a lot with the other chaps. It was good fun." Much of the afternoon John spent listening on Atkins's gramophone to classical music, some of which he and Dorothy had seen interpreted by the Russian Ballet. He missed her terribly. "Tonight I need you so much," a sentiment he shared letter after letter. "My longing makes the time ahead until we are together so very long indeed. Darling, as I think what grand times we will have I am so thankful for our sublime Burnham time."

A drive of about a hundred miles with Atkins through the New Forest and surrounding countryside put him in a poetic mood.

The autumn coloring although far less vivid than in your land was very beautiful. A leaden sky & a misty day were appropriate settings for the fading summer glories. The forest was similar to Burnham Beeches in parts so very extensive. There were delightful glades, ancient gnarled giants, young straight slender saplings so elegant & graceful, wide open commons covered with heather & gorse bushes, & quaint thatched foresters' cottages.

He so earnestly wished to share the experience with her in person. "But we will return, buy a car & tour England, eschewing the cities."

Sunday evening he exulted. "I have had such a grand day & feel so fit & well for I have had some strenuous exercise." Four of the men had played badminton for two hours, much more vigorous, he reckoned, than tennis. Then three of them, minus "the one resident here who is doleful & a nuisance to himself & his friends," adjourned to the billiard room for snookers. "We ended up by listening to some excellent music in Atkins' room as we had a final drink. A very excellent & welcome change from St. Paul's."

"Yesterday as I was returning," he confided to Dorothy the next day, "I saw a well built girl & commented to myself 'Ha! she is not as good as my wife.' It then struck me how amazing & unreal it was for me to be a married man." He and Dorothy had actually been together so few days that the realization "at times tends to elude me. But I am so proud & thankful that you are really my wife. How I would have liked to have introduced you to my friends over the weekend. How very envious the chaps would have been."

The next weekend, after John's busy Saturday morning in the wards, an Australian friend who had taken his fellowship at Edinburgh with John stopped by.

I went for a run with him in his car then after dinner here we went to a continuous vaudeville show. It was quite good. Since then I have been doing some work. . . . Darling, arrange to have some days off between Christmas & New Year if possible because I want to carry you off & have you all to myself. Such is my 'bedtime' thought as I say goodnight. . . . Come to me in my dreams.

Two young women from Basingstoke, whom he had apparently met during his weekend at Park Prewett, rang him later in London. It was Armistice Day, November 11. He had planned to get the wards done early "and go off to the service at the Cenotaph. How I wish you could accompany me. As it is I am to meet two girls who interest me less than most. One of them suggested I meet them so I had but little option but to do so." Still, the day proved memorable.

John wanted to get as close as he could to the Cenotaph—by definition, a tomb honoring persons buried elsewhere—London's impressive stone monument on Whitehall Road to Great Britain's war dead. He even hoped to catch a glimpse of King George V and to hear the service. But even though they arrived an hour and a half early, he and the girls could not work their way through the crowd.

By using a mirror held high I was able to see most of the ceremony. It was very simple & very impressive. The bands of the various regiments & detachments from each arrived & took up their station in the roadway surrounding the Cenotaph. Just before 11 o'clock wreaths were placed on the steps, then on the first stroke of Big Ben a gun boomed & suddenly a great silence descended upon that vast concourse. The only sound was the rustling of the leaves of a nearby tree. It was an inspiring act of reverence. A prayer was offered, the Lord's Prayer repeated & "O God Our Help in Ages Past" sung. As I stood there I prayed that neither we nor our children should witness the horrors of another war.

He meditated at that moment on how and where Dorothy was observing the two minutes of silence. In the United States, President Roosevelt gave his first Armistice Day address at the Tomb of the Unknown Soldier in Arlington National Cemetery, and the U.S. Post Office issued a special cover to mark the commemoration's fifteenth anniversary, postmarked WASHINGTON, D.C. NOV 11, 11 - AM, 1933.

After Armistice Day lunch at the hospital, John and the two girls attended the original London production of Cole Porter's musical *Nymph Errant* at the Adelphi Theatre.

It is a spectacular play based on the highly improbable story of a highly sophisticated young miss anxious to experience the thrill of sexual intercourse & of her amazing travels with men who "were either idealists or tired business men." She visits Paris, Venice, Athens, Smyrna & Turkey during her wanderings & despite of rather pointed solicitations meets no success until she returns home to North Oxford.

He did not reveal to Dorothy that it was the family gardener who finally obliged. "Gertrude Lawrence's acting was superb, but somehow or other the play left rather a nasty taste in my mouth."

Earlier that summer during the World Economic Conference, London's society press had hinted at a real-life version of the play. Debonair, 50-year-old King Faisal of Iraq attended the conference in person, ostensibly to observe the proceedings and instruct his delegates. The king's deeper desire, implied *Time* magazine secondhand, was "to renew his acquaintance with two of Britain's most photographed beauties: Lady Louis Mountbatten and the Marchioness of Milford Haven, who visited his arid kingdom unescorted last November in search of desert thrills." Later, John may have seen the notice in September that Faisal had died quite suddenly in Berne, Switzerland.

Back at the hospital on Armistice Day, the jovial Kennedy suggested that Kessell and the two girls from Basingstoke join him and a friend for dinner. Then,

again with Kennedy & his "cobber" in command, we went to "The Plough," a famous public house. We saw the girls off to their train in a taxi & returned to the pub. It consists of a rather uninviting room of fairly large dimensions with a bar along one side. It is paneled & has two rather good looking oil paintings on one wall. A staircase leads up to the next floor & takes up considerable space. By ten o'clock the place is packed with a strange crowd of people, mostly men but with a sprinkling of women mostly prostitutes. It was most interesting to study the faces & types. An off duty policeman, a bus driver, a well known novelist (Liam Flattery [O'Flaherty]), a strangely dressed Bohemian, a clerk, a bum, a doctor to name only a few. Thus I saw a little of London that is unknown to the home loving citizen.

To comfort Dorothy, he added hastily, "It was intriguing as a spectacle, but has no attraction for me. Dearest, you need have no fear of me wishing to spend my evenings in any similar place. Give me a fireside & a wife & see how often I wish to go awandering."

One quiet Sunday afternoon, John set aside his medical books and indulged himself with *The Underground of London*,

very intriguing for it tells of the numerous cafes, night clubs, & bars where all types of criminals foregather. Many of these places are situated in this immediate vicinity. It is amazing to think these people are everywhere about & these haunts thriving & yet one sees nothing of them.

That evening, he attended a lecture unrelated to medicine at the Student Movement International Club in Russell Square, where Professor MacMurray spoke on "The relationship between the Christian religion, Communism, & Fascism." "It was a fine address," John thought, "but it all depended upon the speaker's definition of religion. It was stimulating. Darling, as I sat there this evening I thought that soon I will be going to International House [in New York] with you."

On another night Kessell and an Australian friend had seen a charming three-act operetta, originally staged in Berlin but premiered in English at the Drury Lane Theatre that September. "It is called 'Ball at the Savoy.' The color schemes & the dancing were most elaborate. The theme centred around the right of a wife to pay out an unfaithful husband in kind. You would have enjoyed the show." Next day was the Lord Mayor's Show and the installation of a new lord mayor of London. He would see the procession. This, he explained, was a picturesque ceremonial that had persisted for hundreds of years. "The most interesting part . . . was the Lord Mayor's carriage & horses & his own liveried footmen & guard."

In mid-October, on a Saturday evening, John wrote to Dorothy about his busy day,

but not from a work point of view. I had a ring this morning from two Australian girls who had come to London to the see the sister of one of them off by the boat for Australia. One of them, Gwennie Oats, I know very well for she was a sister in one of the Hospitals I was in in Australia. Gwennie brought us a delightful [clotted] cream dish made in Cornwall.

Obligingly, John went along with Gwennie, her friend, and the returnee to the boat train. For the rest of the day he escorted Nurse Gwennie and the other woman about town. "We saw the changing of the Guards, visited London Museum and Westminster Abbey & returned here for lunch. They rested after lunch for a while then visited some friends. Then I took them along to St. Paul's Cathedral." They stayed for dinner, but because of their previous all-night train trip from Cornwall and their return at midnight, they were content to relax and look at some of his photos rather than take in a show.

"Darling," he began the following paragraph,

it is strange, or perchance it is not, still the fact remains people do not interest me as much as they did once. It is you I want too constantly. They did entirely approve of you from your photos & allowed me to talk quite a lot about you. Another change is that I have not the same desire to go places & see things.

A very good friend from his Edinburgh days, en route to London via Dublin and North Wales, wanted John to meet up with him in either place. But John was not at all sad, he told Dorothy, that he could not do so. "Some day we will see those places together. That is what I feel about so many things, they will not become worthwhile till we do them together. Do you ever have such a feeling?"

When Gwennie Oats moved from Cornwall to London shortly thereafter, of course John told Dorothy. On Halloween, "I had decided to go out to a show this evening when an Australian girl rang me up. It was the girl who had been in the hospital with me in Broken Hill & who has come up from Cornwall to nurse in London." He agreed to meet her at the new Piccadilly Circus Underground, the largest underground station in the world, featuring in the main hall brilliantly illuminated showcases displaying the merchandise of London's finest shops. A world map set off pridefully in a distinctive color all the dominions and colonies of the British Empire. While John waited, he studied the clock that told the time in various parts of the world. "It was 9 o'clock here & 3 o'clock [p.m.] in New Jersey. I wondered what you were actually doing, either at one of your schools or perhaps visiting a patient."

And then, interrupting his thoughts, there was Gwennie. That night John took his sociable friend to see *The Cuckoo in the Nest*, which he considered a bad movie made from a perfectly good play. The plot, which he did not elaborate to Dorothy, centered on a man and a woman in an overcrowded inn forced to share a room together. Previously engaged, each had in the meantime married someone else, which made for lively dialogue. After the movie, John escorted Gwennie back to her hotel, "& then took a brisk half an hour walk back here. It is a lovely clear moonlight night. As I walked Darling, I am lonesome & out of tune with the people here." But then, really, why mention to Dorothy in a single paragraph an old girl friend and the moonlight? He simply shared everything.

Gwennie was on John's arm again the next week as they watched one of England's most renowned actors reprise his role in *The Wandering Jew*. "Matheson Lang took the part of the Jew. His acting was superb. The whole play was well staged & well acted. I enjoyed it immensely. Just think," he enthused to Dorothy, who surely had taken previous note of the willing Nurse Gwennie, "in a very few weeks we will be able to go together to see some of the Broadway shows." Lang, in fact, had played the part in a previous silent movie and again taken the lead when the play had opened on Broadway in 1927.

Plays and movies lifted John's spirits, which rose and fell often during the three-month separation from his wife. (As my sister and I grew up with him, first in New Jersey and later in California, we knew our father as a beautifully even-tempered, kind, and gentle doctor, quick to chuckle and ever with a twinkle in his eye.) His time alone in London, however, tried his basic good nature. Writing as often as he did, he admitted even his bad moods. "Darling, this waiting is the very devil."

Whenever he felt out of sorts, John routinely went for a swim at the YMCA, took a long walk, or read a detective novel. "I felt a little fed up towards dinner time so I went across & had a swim. I felt lots better & did some studying this evening." "If you had been close by I would have worried you whatever you had been doing to come & play with me & tease me back into a good humour. Darling, you will have such a lot to put up with when you actually have me on your hands."

Feelings of eager anticipation of life in America alternated with fears that he might not measure up to her expectations as he perceived them. Ever waiting for her next letter kept him anxious, "but when I think of our few wonderful hours I live for the future. Darling, my aim in life now is to live to the fullest & to be of use in the world. Only with you & through you can I do this." Some days he felt especially able. "When I feel so Hercules-like, wouldn't you like to be here to receive such a hug as I could give? The trouble is I have no desire to test out my strength on anyone else. It must be you or no one."

On Tuesday morning, September 26, writing from his cramped little room, John confessed to her,

Mine is not an impatient nature but one cannot help but long for the time when we will be together. We have so much to do & then to be working for "us" & "ours." It is a wonderful future. I am so confident of what I can do with your help & encouragement. Never was a man more fortunate than myself. Darling, to know we belong to each other is consoling. I must away to work, Dearest.

Later the same day, that confidence had worn thin. "I have felt unsettled & discontented this evening. I could not settle to anything. The one person I wanted & still long for is not at hand. At times the desire is so very great."

Glancing up from paper and pen on another evening, John marveled, "It seems almost unreal to think that it is really my wife's photo I am looking at." She was smiling back at him. "Darling, your faith in me helps me more than you can ever know. Seven weeks ago you said 'Yes' to me. What lots have happened since then & what grand times we have in store." Still, John reminded her, he surely would falter.

Oh, I have my work cut out & so much to accomplish. When I realize how very ordinary I am & how little I know, I am afeared. Darling, I am depending on you so very much for moral support & encouragement. Your faith in me is a thing I am amazed at yet how it helps me for I am determined not to fail you.

John so wanted her reassurance, asking one early November morning,

Darling, you will still love me when you discover I am not much good at anything, won't you? For I will need you so very much & to know I had lost your respect & love would be crushing indeed. It will always be a puzzle to me to know what you saw in me but that is unimportant except that I must always keep that interest alive, the important thing is that you do love me & I do love you. Darling, I must away & do my wards.

He admitted to an occasional bout of peevishness. "I wonder if you will get tired of me & annoyed with me when I have such peevish moods as the present one. They do not come often or last long I assure you." On another occasion, "Me thinks it is well nigh time I left here for I find myself getting peevish & annoyed very easily, a state unusual to me. I must reform before I join you." Then, a couple of days later, "My indifference & peevishness has vanished. What the cause of it was I do not know but I do know I am relieved to be myself again."

An uncharacteristically visceral passion gripped him one night as he recalled their arrival eleven weeks earlier at Burnham Lodge.

I feel unsettled & uncertain. It is a time when I need you with me. I need you to help me see the zest & the thrill of living. Why I should have such a "flat" feeling I know not. The day has gone fairly well & I have been to a show this evening. Perchance my state is largely explained by my longing for my own woman & by my disinclination for any substitute. My Woman, you have a very large place to occupy in my life. I will not be completely happy until I have done things that prove to you I am as good at my job as you think me. I know you have no doubt but that is not enough. Do you ever feel in the mood for fierce love making [with] rather primitive instinctive feelings urging you on? The mood in which men hurt the one they love. It is rather new to me. Dear Sweetheart, thank God you too are passionate. Things will go well with us. Storms of many kinds will sweep over us but together we will weather them & enjoy the times of peace & calm all the more. Goodnight, Wife of Mine. I feel very possessive tonight & strangely jealous of you. You are my mate & I am lonesome for you. Sweet dreams, Beloved. Your lover, John.

5

COMING TO AMERICA
IMMIGRATION AND BOARD EXAMS

John never expressed any doubts about moving to the United States. He seems to have decided, based on his earlier experiences—only hinted at in his letters—that America was the place for him. Marriage to Dorothy sealed the bargain. He even allowed that, after comparing British and U.S. urology, "I find that all that I have to say is in favor of American urology." He greatly admired Dr. S. R. Woodruff of Bayonne, New Jersey, "a thorough gentleman & the man I would model myself on," envisioning a partnership with him one day. He asked Dorothy to call on Dr. Woodruff, whom he considered his best hope for securing a job in the U.S. "His office is just off the big square near the underground station in Jersey City. I could take [you] there much easier than direct you to the place."

Just as soon as he disembarked again in America, they must get away, just the two of them, for several days, to anywhere she pleased.

I have only been to Atlantic City for one day when I was in Philadelphia. Make any arrangements you like so long as we are away together, mountains, plains, or sea are only minor considerations. I do ask for somewhere to wander though & away from the maddening crowd if such be possible.

He recalled vividly the fall colors in New England, but knew he would not arrive in time. "Next year," he hoped in mid-October, "maybe we can take a few days off & go north into the mountains about this time of the year."

John was in no way estranged from his family in Australia; America simply offered greater promise for the future. His clergyman father and his mother, both 70 years old, wrote lovingly to him in London congratulating him and Dorothy on their marriage. He enclosed their letters and sent them on to her.

How eagerly they must have awaited news & how commonplace my letters in between would be. I know something about waiting for "longed for" letters. Darling, if we can possibly arrange for mother & father to visit us or for us to visit them we must do so. They would so dearly like to welcome their new daughter & how proud I would be to take you, Beloved.

His accomplished big brother, Stephen L. Kessell, known as "Dex" or "Kim," two years his senior and a graduate of Oxford University, was by 1933 conservator of forests in Western Australia. "Yesterday I received a letter from my brother. He sent rather guarded congratulations to me & said he would wait till he heard something more before congratulating you. He does not seem sure that you are so lucky. I wonder." Dex had only one child, "a little girl Julie by name."

The Kessell Family, about 1920: The Rev. Stephen and Alice, and their children (left to right) Enid, Stephen L., Marjory, and John S. (courtesy Bob Cleland)

John's sisters, both nurses in Australia, were delighted. He also enclosed letters from them, which had reached him in early October. Marjory, a jolly soul and youngest of the four Kessell children, cheered, "John Dear, Aren't you a great big surprise! . . . congratulations, old Dear, & the best of luck to you both. Do hurry up & write telling us all about the wedding & please send some photos or snaps quickly." Enid, who considered him her closest sibling, mailed two letters to him in London, both dated the same day. "Am longing to meet your wife," she wrote in the first. "Of course if you chose her, I shall love your choice, for our tastes are similar, aren't they?"

Enid's second letter, on stationery from Adelaide Children's Hospital, which John did not forward to Dorothy, was anguished. She had not intended to write, "preferring rather that we should discuss it when we met." Now, however, with John going on to the United States, she chose to put her quandary in a letter to him. She was deeply in love with a married man. The man's wife, ten years his senior, had long since abandoned him in all but name yet refused a divorce. Only Marjory and a few friends knew of Enid's requited love. Dex, who was not privy to the depth of the affair, "likes him awfully." With the man's reluctant help, she now planned to escape temporarily to England. "To leave takes a great deal of courage, but the fact that I should have you there, whom you know I love dearly, has helped considerably."

Sympathetic but "much perturbed," John wrote to his new wife the same day he received Enid's letters. "Once again I have been a blind-eyed, self-centered fool." His sister's love was no mere infatuation. Enid "is a girl very much after your own heart. When you know her you will love her. Enid is very dear to me & I must find some way to help her all that is in my power." It was obvious to him that his sister would need their long-term moral support and encouragement. "Knowing you as I do, Wife-of-Mine, I do not hesitate to use the inclusive 'we.'" He would think on paper and see what conclusions occurred to him.

Even if Enid could reach London before John sailed, a brief meeting would hardly suffice. But if she stayed on in Australia for six months or a year, then visited England and came on to America, he and Dorothy would be settled. Or if Enid arrived in England on January 18, as she planned, she could take a nursing job for a year, at the end of which "we would have an idea of how we stood & might be able to arrange for her to come across & get a job or at any rate stay some time near us." By then she would know whether she wished to go back to Australia.

"Have no fear," he reassured Dorothy, "that my thoughts & worries about Enid make you less precious or less necessary to me. It is just the opposite. In our great good fortune I would stretch out a real helping hand, but my hand alone is not half so strong as our hand." He would inquire next day about ships arriving from Australia before he left, then cable Enid. He asked Dorothy for any suggestions she might have about the matter. He was so thankful that they had found each other free, had married, and could openly share their joy with others. "Your love for me impels me to strive to help anyone less fortunate. . . . Without you as my guiding-star & the centre of my life I should not wish to live. But for you, my love knows no limitations, [and I] would dare & if necessary die."

Dorothy's response heartened him. If he needed to stay on to comfort Enid, she would understand. "I knew you would write exactly as you have done but confirmation of our oneness & of our mutual willingness to forego our own pleasures & longings to help someone less fortunate is very helpful." (As things worked out, Enid arrived in London early in 1934, took training there, and later went to the United States for a three-month course in dietetics at Orange Memorial Hospital in East Orange. She eventually returned to Australia to marry her love and raise a family.)

Within a week of Dorothy's August sailing, her new husband had begun worrying about the process of immigration. In the 1920s the United States had adopted a national origins quota system by which each nationality was assigned an annual quota based on its representation in the 1920 U.S. census. The State Department then distributed the requisite number of visas through United States embassies and consulates abroad. John cannot have known how drastically the global depression had slashed demand for U.S. visas. Between 1932 and 1936, more people left the country than entered. Even the smallest quotas went unfulfilled in 1933, a year when U.S. officials processed only a trickle of 23,000 immigrants coming to America. Dr. Kessell need not have worried. Everything favored him— he was white, English-speaking and from a favored country, a skilled professional, and married to a responsible U.S. citizen.

When he explained at the American Consulate that "I was married to an American—I did not stress what a wonderful one—they said for you to get in touch with the nearest immigration office & notify them of the fact & to tell them I wish to enter on the quota." Someone at the consulate typed a note for him, which he enclosed in his letter to Dorothy: "File with immigration authorities/nearest place of residence Form 633 on your behalf as the husband of an American citizen."

Furthermore, they explained at the consulate, it might be possible for him to enter the country even without a job if Immigration was satisfied that his wife could support him, "so that I should not [be] a burden to the State." She should file a financial statement from her banker indicating the size of her practice. He would nevertheless write Dr. Woodruff about a job. Once Dorothy had John's letter in hand, she hastened to fill out a U.S. affidavit of support supplied by the Cunard and Anchor Lines.

While John found the possibility of entering without a job "cheering" in one sense, that certainly was not his intention. "Dear One," he wrote on September 20, "I am most anxious to have a job right away. . . . I have written to Dr. Woodruff, Dr. Pelonge & the Chicago Medical Bureau on the subject." Pondering the matter a week later, he responded to her apparent offer of personal financial support:

> Darling, how I do love you for making our future such a grand partnership, for so freely sharing all you have. I do not think I will be in need of any money, thank you, for when I hear from my brother the limit of my limited resources in Australia I will have him send me some straightaway.

John loved the idea of their family partnership, yet he would never shirk the role of breadwinner.

It is absolutely essential, for as a husband I needs must make enough to support my wife & keep the children to be . . . for I simply have to give her beautiful clothes, send her lots of flowers, have elegant & tasteful things in the home, be able to take her out to dance, to sup & to the play. Not that she demands such things, she does not, but such things are her right & have them she shall.

He had written also to a Mr. Don in New York City. Don and his wife were personal friends, and by the end of September he had received "a delightful letter from Mr. Don, the Australian Representative in New York, congratulating me & extending a very cordial invitation for us both to visit them when I arrive. You will enjoy them."

John had been back again to the American Consulate to ask about customs. "Except for my personal belongings, my books & any instruments that I possess, I will have to pay duty on everything I bring." As a noncitizen, he could not claim the $100 exemption. Hence, he saw no point in anyone giving them a gift that he had to pay duty on. Any household belongings more than a year old would be admitted free. "Incidently the linen I bring in will be taxed. We should have made sure you had your $100 worth. Still if that is our only worry we will be fortunate."

He was able to report happily in early October, "A Cunard Company man arrived with copies of your affidavit." Again the ball was in John's court. "I must now see the American Consul." He would try to make an appointment the next day. "I want to be sure everything is in order before I am interviewed. When he says he understands & that I may enter how overjoyed will I be. Shall I invite him to visit us or shall I suggest he call me in if he develops an enlarged prostate?"

THE CUNARD AND ANCHOR LINES

United States of America

AFFIDAVIT OF SUPPORT

STATE OF _New Jersey_ } s. s.

COUNTY OF _Essex_

PREPAID TICKET NO. _____

(1) I, _Dorothy Luttridge Kessell_ being duly sworn, depose and say:

(2) That I am _33_ years of age and was born at _East Orange, New Jersey_

(3) That my present address is _43 South Maple Ave_ Street, City of _East Orange_ County of _Essex_ State of _New Jersey_

(4) That I have resided in the United States for the past _____ years having been legally admitted for permanent residence at the port (station) of _____ ex S. S. (R. R.) _____ _____, _____, _____; holding American Consular Visa No. _____ issued at
_____ month _____ day _____ year
on _____

(5) That I am a citizen of the United States holding Certificate of Naturalization No. _____ issued at _____ by the _____ Court on _____ month _____ day _____ year

(6) That I have declared my intention to become a citizen of the United States and hold Declaration of Intention Certificate No. _____ issued at _____ on _____ month _____ day _____ year

(7) That it is my intention and desire to have the following relative(s) or friend(s) at present residing at _St Pauls Hospital, Endell St, London W.C.2, England_ come and remain with me in the United States until they become self supporting.

(8) That it is my intention and desire to have the following relative(s) or friend(s) now residing at _____ come to the United States for a temporary visit not to exceed _____ months and that I am able and willing to furnish a bond of $500 to the United States Immigration Authorities to insure (his) (her) (their) departure at the expiration of such period should bond be required.

Name of Alien	Age	Sex	Relationship	Place and Date of Birth
Dr John Samuel Kessell	34	m.	Husband	Australia, July 29. 99

(9) That my (husband's) occupation is _____ that my (husband's) average weekly earnings are $_____

(10) That I possess property aggregating: Real Estate $_____ Personal $_____

(11) That my dependents consist of _____

(12) That I hereby agree and guarantee to send to school those herein named who have not yet reached the age of sixteen, and that they shall be kept at school until they have reached such age, and that no aliens herein named shall be placed at work unsuitable to their years.

(13) That I am willing and able to receive, maintain and support all those herein mentioned, and do hereby guarantee to save harmless the United States or any State, city, village or township thereof against any aliens herein mentioned becoming a public charge.

(14) That this affidavit is made by me for the information of the American Consul in connection with the application for visas filed by the above-mentioned aliens and for the information of the Immigration Authorities at the port of arrival in the United States.

Witness _Mrs. H. H. Hewen_

Address _73 Carnegie Ave._
East Orange, N. J.

Dorothy Luttridge Kessell
(Signature of Deponent)

Subscribed and sworn to before me, a Notary Public in and for said County

on this _15th_ day

of _Sept_ A. D., 19_33_

Clarence S Johnson
(Notary Public)

My commission expires _April 25, 1938_

C 319 T. C. 72039

Printed in U. S.

Dorothy's Affidavit of Support

But further inquiry dampened his spirits. The Cunard shipping people had led John to believe that all he had to do was make an appointment. Consular officials, however, told him that he must "wait longer until they receive word from Washington. I hope it will not be long for I want things fixed up." A week later, he had notice "to apply for the preference quota." He would do so immediately and hoped all the pieces would fall into place by the end of the following week. "It will be a relief."

Sunday, October 15: "a splendid autumn day, such a one to pack a hamper & over the hills & far away especially from hospital. . . . Won't it be grand," he offered eagerly, "to have a quota number in my pocket?" Although he had his passport photos in hand and a duplicate marriage certificate from Wesley's Chapel, John admitted to Dorothy later, on "a dull wet cheerless morning [that] I am a little fearful of the interview for so much depends on it." Finally it was set: 11:00 a.m., Thursday, November 2. The outcome prompted a second letter that evening.

"This is an extra special letter. I do wish I could rush it across to you. Truly Thursday is our especial day for I received my visa today. Just fancy I have a free permit of entry. Isn't it grand?" Now he could consult the sailing schedules with gusto, assured that he could be with her in East Orange by Christmas. En route back to the hospital, "I walked along with my chest thrown out & a feeling that I was ready to face all comers. Apparently a doubt has lurked in my mind but it is gone now for I have my quota number." The interview had gone well.

I was not cross questioned at all save that the Vice Consul thought the physician must refer to me. I explained the matter. I was very fortunate that there happened to be an Australian number over here, otherwise it would have meant cabling for one. As soon as I have fixed upon a ship I will let you know.

In any case make the Christmas pudding large enough for me to have a big helping. I will be mighty hungry after my long trip.

What a Christmas they would have! Feeling a bit frisky, he ventured in the same letter, "What does it matter if you have wobbly eyes, a crooked nose & are pigeon toed, I love you just the same. But, oh Darling, you haven't got any of those things. You are just right in every way. Gosh, how I do want you. What a time you are in for." They deserved more honeymoons. "Perhaps you have not noticed my attitude. I am rather good at hiding my feelings. But wait until I have the chance to act, then there will be no hiding the fact. Darling, I do love you so."

John was charmed that Dorothy's mother had written to him in London "to make me feel that it is my home that awaits me." Saddened, however, that he would not be there to offer his support as she went in for an eye operation, he knew it would be successful. Although he and Dorothy were far apart, their love for each other far outweighed any inconvenience.

The difference it has made to me is something that I marvel at frequently. Life is very wonderful & so very worthwhile nowadays. The future holds such untold happiness in store for us. I am so anxious to take my place at the table & to take my turn at lighting the fire & cooking the breakfast & really be one of the family. What a change from hospital life & living in lodgings.

In response to another letter from his mother-in-law, John thanked her for taking the trouble. "But it seems to me mothers are the same the world over, they think of their children first & themselves last or not at all." Both their mothers had birthdays in November. "What times we will have when I join the family circle," he went on. "I warn you, I tend towards obesity & Dorothy does not like fat men, so you will have to refrain from overfeeding me. I am sure to come to you if Dorothy cuts down my food for the sake of my figure." He wished that Mother Alice could enjoy the beauty of England.

Alongside his previous worries about immigration, John confessed to Dorothy a recurring anxiety about the national and state board exams he would face in the U.S. He had a folder from the National Board of Medical Examinations. "I have written back asking whether I can be exempt from Part I & what verification of the work I have done & exams passed will be required. If I have to send to Australia I wish to know straightaway." He learned that the New Jersey State Board held exams only in October and June and thought, given that schedule, he should probably take the national exams first. "Dearest," he reminded her on October 13, "you will not forget to send me that book of questions set in the National Board exams? When I look at the syllabus I realize how little I do know about some things. Still with you coaching me I should have little enough to worry about."

New York State held its medical board exams three times a year, the next one from January 29 through February 1, 1934, which seemed good to him. "Also there is a clause that talks about license by endorsement & includes foreign universities. I might possibly be able to gain a license that way. I will write tomorrow & ask." The secretary of the National Board had agreed to "bring my case before someone or other & maybe I would be exempt from Part I. It would be the very devil if I could not get that exemption. Still we will see." A response from the Medical Bureau of Philadelphia suggested that he first establish himself as a doctor in the U.S., then put his name on their books for a possible job. Not having heard from Dr. Woodruff also concerned him.

In the meanwhile, he wrote to his old school and to the University of Adelaide for certified statements of the work he had done in Australia, pre-medical and medical. Dorothy had sent him forms that he was having trouble filling out, "as our educational system does not run absolutely parallel with yours. I can only hope the data I get will be sufficient for it takes so long to get replies from Australia." Toward the end of October,

the examination papers & Gaepps questions & answers duly arrived. If I have to take exams in Chemistry, Anatomy, Physiology & Materia Medica it will be just too bad for I have forgotten so much about those subjects. Medicine, Surgery, Gynae & Hygiene will be bad enough. As there is no getting away from so doing, that is that.

The same evening he "felt absolutely fed up to the teeth." He tried to get into a show, but could not, "so I went for a long walk, four or five miles, & felt lots better."

When finally he had a letter from Dr. Woodruff, there was little cause to rejoice. John enclosed it for Dorothy to read for herself. "My dear Kessell," wrote Woodruff, explaining first that he had been away and then congratulating the Australian on his marriage. "I know Mrs. Kessell must be very fine & sweet and I'm sure she is to be congratulated in obtaining a fine fellow like yourself." The New Jersey doctor listed the vacancies for urologists that had already been filled, then lamented the sad general state of medicine in Depression-era America. At Bayonne Hospital everything was free. "Of course that's good for the Resident but it isn't so hot for me. Things have never been so bad in medicine in this country before. Nobody seems to have any money. However I guess it's the same way all over & we must try to make the best of it."

University of Adelaide Medical School graduates, 1923
(J. S. Kessel[l], top row left)

Between 1929 and 1933, American physicians' incomes had dropped on average nearly 50 percent. Many people, especially the poor, put off seeing a doctor indefinitely, and those patients who intended to pay their medical bills often paid them last. Empty beds, unpaid bills, and the inability of charitable organizations to raise funds threatened hospitals. Yet despite such glum circumstances, Dr. Woodruff encouraged John to come ahead. "Get over as soon as you can. Mrs. W. sends her greetings."

Four days before he embarked for the States, John had a more hopeful letter from Dorothy. "You are such a Dear. I received a splendid letter from you today telling me that you thought there was plenty of space for a urologist in East Orange. It will be rather grand fun, won't it?" She had further raised his spirits. "I sincerely hope you are right in thinking that I may escape having to sit [for] the State Board exams. On Monday I will get as many testimonials as possible."

John wanted to look presentable when he came ashore. Late in October, he had ordered new suits and an overcoat, wishing that she were there to help him pick out the material. "I feel I must be a credit to you & I have no clothes to be proud of at present. The overcoat should be a beauty & warm. I went to a Jewish tailor who does his own tailoring. He has no shop but works at home. I hope he makes a good job of my clothes."

Then a week later he asked her, "What about a trip with me to the East End to visit my Jewish tailor? You cannot possibly fit it in? Well I will have to go with old Phil." He and "old Phil," not identified further, did go. "The overcoat," he predicted again,

will be a beauty & the suits things to be proud of. He is an artist at his game. I told him how very well my wife dressed & that I must not let her down by my appearance. He assured me he would take extra trouble & that there would be absolutely no fear of that. Darling, I am so proud of you & do love you so.

6

OTHER WOMEN

My father loved women. And they loved him. Yet by his very openness—seemingly oblivious to the prospect of jealousy on the part of his new wife—he gave ample evidence that he was indeed faithful to her. Not that the chance to stray was ever far off for the companionable Australian doctor. One evening in mid-October, for example, the matron had four free theater tickets for her, two of the nurses, and him. After the show, he invited the three women to join him for supper.

Matron asked to be excused so we saw her home. At the door one of the sisters developed excuses. I think she thought she was being very kind to the other girl & myself. We went off for supper & I quite enjoyed yarning but how little that sister understood. Just as you enjoy men's company still, so I do that of women, but how flat it is.

Both John and Dorothy had previous significant others, hers called Charles, his Gwen (not Gwennie Oats). The first hint of her former involvement was his mere "P.P.S. Poor Charles. Lucky John." Charles, however, was unduly persistent, causing John to comment,

Of course we will go dancing & I will become so proficient that you will wish to dance with me for the sake of my dancing as well as because I am your beloved. Charles seems to be making a nuisance of himself. I hope your letter has acted as a final deterrent. I am only perturbed that he should be behaving so annoyingly & worrying you. No, Charles & I would & will not agree.

John, again with free tickets, went to the theater on Monday evening, October 9; when he returned,

I found a letter from Gwen, the girl I left behind in Australia, in all sense of the word. She sent us congratulations. I do not think she had any regrets at our marriage, rather was she relieved at the complete & final termination of her & my own relationship. She sent a farewell to my old self. I hope she will remain or become a friend of the new "us."

One Sunday afternoon, John told Dorothy that "he threw away numerous collected letters," some presumably from previous girlfriends. "It was with mixed feeling I destroyed some of them. Be assured there was no shadow of a regret that it was not any one of the writers. No,

Darling, I am so proud of you & have not ceased to wonder that you should have chosen me. It is amazing, Dear One."

As he described his pleasant weekend in late August with Lil Walsh, Stella, and Auntie at the Swan Hotel in Petworth, the newly married John, innocently but foolishly, included in his love letters to Dorothy details he might have spared her. He need not have described, for example, Lil's emotional response to his marriage, nor his chance encounter next morning.

> Darling, just as I came out of the bathroom along came such a nice lass to go in but I was not interested. Now if it had been a dark-haired, brown-eyed girl with dimples & such dear features me thinks I would have turned back with her. Would you blame me doing so with such a lass?

Norah Marsh, one of his women friends whom Dorothy had met in London, rang him a week after the wedding wanting "to know all about our doings at Canterbury. Just fancy that." The following Friday, he got in late. "Guess whom I have been to see. Yes, our friend Norah. She is a dear & so very interesting. My Word! what close friends you & Norah would become if we lived near her." From nine that evening, "we yarned on & on as I sipped her very excellent sherry. She sent her love to you & wished to hear all about things. Do not be alarmed, I did not bore her with my chattering about ourselves. I did enjoy my evening though."

Another woman, young Janet, also telephoned him. "She was thrilled by you & thought you ever so nice. She said she could sit & listen to you talk for hours. In her own naive way she was unstinting in her praise & very genuine." Janet's sister was going to Germany as governess to two children, and Janet thought she might go also as the baby's nursemaid. "How I tremble for Janet's future. She really is such a child & an adorable one." If the weather was decent the next Wednesday, John would go for a swim with Janet.

The weather may not have cooperated, for that Wednesday evening after "another busy, busy day," Janet came by the hospital for dinner. "She is refreshing company, so naive & genuine. She delights to talk about you & is thrilled with our marriage." Since she was scheduled to leave for Germany in two weeks, she had much else to talk about. After dinner they looked at snapshots of Petworth House, and he promised Dorothy that he would send some to New Jersey. Later Janet went with him to deliver a parcel to the two Australian girls Lil and Stella, "then Jan helped me put snaps in an album, one of Scotch views. The child sent lots of messages to you. That she was looking after me for you, that she hopes we will be ever so happy & so on."

With the exception of six stainless steel dinner knives given to them by Mr. Thompson, most of the gifts they received were from women, particularly the nurses at St. Paul's Hospital.

Darling, do you remember meeting a nurse just as Janet was leaving, Nurse Brooks. I introduced her to you. Well she and another nurse—Nurse Jones—gave [us] such a beautiful set of fish knives & forks. I am enclosing the note. You will write them a note, won't you? I am enclosing the list of people. It is a very long & varied one. I hope you can understand most of the addresses.

When he opened a mysterious gift of a child's toy pram and one wee doll—noting that the pram would hold two babies—he suspected the nurses.

Part way into another letter, in which he was praising at length his wife's charms, he hesitated, adding in parentheses:

(Nurse Brooks just came into the room. She sent you her love, & said to tell you my behavior has been exemplary since you left as far as she knows. I can add that there has been no incentive for me to be otherwise. Darling, you have given me something very wonderful, unobtainable with anyone else.)

Returning to the hospital one night after a date with Norah in mid-September, John ran into his colleague Kennedy, who asked him what Dorothy "would say to me going out. I assured him I was about to tell you all about it. His remark was 'Telling your wife things is one of the pitfalls of married life.' I disagreed with him. I am a married life and he is not, so I should know." John had gone to Norah's for a sherry, then she joined him for dinner at his favorite Japanese restaurant. They had sukiyaki at the table, where he displayed his skills as cook and surgeon with chopsticks. "Norah ate with chopsticks also. It was quite good fun. She is such a dear & encourages me to talk about you & our plans, not that I need much urging. We sat on in the restaurant until after ten o'clock, then I saw Norah home & walked back here."

John sometimes wrote of women friends in a most mundane context. After a full morning in the wards, at 12:30 Vera Gaetzens, "a very good friend of mine called to see me. She asked for your address & will write you." He did not say about what. "She was one person I did want you to meet. She stayed to lunch. After lunch a friend came in to have a TAB [typhoid-paratyphoid] injection & I took a Wass[ermann blood sample, to test for syphilis]. That reminds me my own W.R. was negative."

When three photos of Dorothy arrived, John immediately showed them off. "Me thinks I have amused the hospital by the proud way I have shown your photos to those I think anything of here." He thought it ironic, however, that he did not have them in his possession as he wrote to her that evening.

Just before my session I took them to show the lady almoner [social service worker]—a very interesting woman who is vastly intrigued by our doings. I left them in her keeping while I did the session. When I returned for them after dinner she had gone & very carefully locked them away. She knew how precious they are to me. Truly a tragi-comedy.

At the same time, he referred to another woman as if Dorothy knew who she was. "Darling, I had a letter from Helen Bolman this evening. It was a very nice one hoping I would be very happy. I feel it was a difficult one for her to write. I did appreciate it."

Another Friday morning, September 22, John told Dorothy he would be meeting two Danish girls the next day. "It should be interesting & I enjoy acting as a guide to London especially to people of other nations. I believe it is their first visit." He got in late Saturday night "after rather a strenuous afternoon's sightseeing followed by a show. The two Danish girls are two nice, keenly interested, healthy lasses." He had just a little headache. He so wanted his wife. He knew she would forgive him if he put off telling her about his afternoon until the next day. "I am fit & well, only I want to lie down beside you, to be near you, to rest & recuperate."

Not until Tuesday evening did John recount his afternoon with the Danish girls. It had rained the entire time. They had begun at the

Houses of Parliament "where we yarned to the same Policeman at the top of Westminster Hall," and sloshed back along the Embankment to the Middle and Inner Temple, viewing the Halls and the Temple Church, then out into the Strand, and to the old Roman Bath. They arrived too late to see the Wallace Collection, a museum of fine and decorative arts, so they had tea instead.

The happy threesome then walked to Piccadilly Circus and had a look around the showy Underground station. An innovation for subway commuters that year, 1933, was a free pocket edition of a supremely simple diagrammatic, out-of-scale map of the system conceived by Harry Beck, an unemployed electrical draftsman. The concept still guides travelers on the Tube today. From Piccadilly, the trio headed back to the Strand and a Japanese restaurant for sukiyaki. "The girls were highly delighted with it. We went to see 'Richard of Bordeaux,' a very excellent historical play based on the life of Richard III [II]. It was admirably acted. Darling, you know my thoughts tonight."

Admirably acted indeed. This was the very play, opening at the New Theatre the previous February, that catapulted 27-year-old John Gielgud to stardom. London's *Daily Express* proclaimed Gielgud "the supreme idol of the pit and the gallery, where most of the intelligent playgoers sit." Alec Guinness claimed to have seen the play more than a dozen times, captivated by Gielgud's "fabulous voice . . . like a silver trumpet muffled in silk." A month after John and the two Danish girls had seen the play, he received a package from them, an exquisite little porcelain dish. "It is sent to us. Wasn't it charming of them?"

At her desk in New Jersey, Dorothy must have written to John on the subject of socializing with members of the opposite sex. "Of course," he replied, "I approve of your policy of not dashing about with all & sundry but Darling I trust you so implicitly that I know that you will only choose to accompany friends as I would wish you to have." Farther down in the same letter, he returned to the theme.

"Darling, it does make such a difference knowing you feel as I do, that you look forward to my letters as I do to yours, that you are interested to meet people as I am but that they really do not count & that you live for me as I do for you." It was Thursday, their day.

Such exquisite soul-satisfying contentment & bliss we found in each other's company. We have fragrant beautiful memories that will remain with us forever. They will be so helpful when the road is rough. Darling, we are indeed fortunate that our married life has led us into a garden so fair.

When next he rang Norah, her mother told him that Norah was not well and that her doctor had prescribed rest for the remainder of the week. "I offered to call if she so desired & have a yarn. This morning I sent some roses from us. I will ring again tomorrow." In bed for a week with an infection, Norah dropped him a line at the hospital saying that she hoped to be up by the weekend and asking him to please thank Dorothy for her card and note.

Never did John fail to cushion mention of his women friends in London with heartfelt expressions of love for her.

Some time I must take some days off & tell you the charms & attainments of my beloved. It is no simple matter to do so for she is as complex as she is adorable, for she is all woman & then she is an efficient doctor too, charming host & provocative coquette. Was ever a man so fortunate? What is a little waiting & a few thousand miles when one is actually married and what is most important beloved by such a one.

He awakened on the morning of October 2, hoping that Dorothy was "'fresh as a daisy' & as impish as ever. Ho! my own merry Puck I would like to be within striking distance of your merry wit. Still soon I will have the arduous task of spanking you when you play your pranks upon me. Don't you quake at the threat?"

Dear Wife of Mine, our love is a much greater thing than a mere physical oneness, it is something far vaster, it is of things infinite, a spiritual thing & that is why we both of us are rather scared of the immensity of it at times. Darling, despite the annoyance caused by the Atlantic at present we have something wonderful to be thankful for.

John kept all her letters (which later were lost). During spare moments, he read and reread his wife's words and felt close to her.

We are going to look forward to the long winter nights when we will be together. There is so much we can read together, discuss & learn, all sorts of subjects to explore together. What fun it will be to be pals in every sense of the word. It would be sad to be married to someone who was not a companion intellectually as well as otherwise. What a wonderful future stretches out ahead of us.

He was counting the days until their first Christmas together. He asked partly in jest, "About Christmas cards, Dearest, if I get some printed from Dr. & Mrs. Kessell, or should I have Dr. & Mrs. Dr. Kessell?" Although he was certainly proud that his wife was also a doctor, the latter did not look right to him. (Later, as they practiced medicine together, she was professionally Dr. Lottridge and socially Mrs. Kessell.) He was happy to let his wife worry about Christmas presents. "Ah yes, it is a fine institution this marriage business when you have the right people together. Darling, two of the 'right' people are separated by an ocean but the finest Christmas present the other will get will be each other."

7

"COME AT ONCE!"

B y the last days of October, Dorothy's patience was wearing thin. She longed for John as much as he for her. Her friends, even her parents, must have begun asking, "Well, when *is* he coming?" Yet all the while, John assured his new wife that he was lonesome for her and out of sorts with people in London.

> I am so anxious to start anew for that is what it really does mean. I only half enjoy things nowadays & find my interest slight where it used to be wholehearted. Darling, there is no doubt at all that loving you & being your husband & having you as my wife is a whole-time & a man's job. And I am the man. Lucky fellow (chorus).

In answer to Dorothy's earlier query about what ship he might take, he replied he would likely be aboard the Cunard Line's *Carinthia* sailing December 14. Still, it may have seemed to her that he was not acting decisively enough, that he was staying busy with work, his friends' problems, and a jolly London social life.

And who, Dorothy must have wondered, was this Gwennie Oats, John's Australian "girl friend," the one he "knew very well," so quick with congratulations and a Cornish-cream dish, the woman her husband was escorting about town to plays and movies? John had mentioned Nurse Oats's move from Cornwall to London on October 31. As the envelope containing his letters written from October 28 to November 1 made its way on the six- to eight-day crossing and then the short mail hop from New York City to 43 South Maple Avenue, John and Gwennie saw another play. "Isn't it great," he rhapsodized to Dorothy, "that we will be able to talk about Piccadilly & the shows running there & both know the places & be able to visualize them. It will be so much better than one telling the other."

Dorothy's abrupt, unexplained cable arrived late Tuesday, November 14. It read simply, "Come at once!" "Darling," he wrote at 2:00 a.m., "your cable has mystified me. I can't make out whether there is a job or a chance of one or what is in the offing." He thought of telephoning her, but $30.00 for three minutes seemed a bit much. "As I said in my [return] cable I can leave anytime if needs be. If I had nothing to lose I should like to stay out my time as I agreed. I am all 'at sea' until I hear from you again." But he had a premonition. "Darling," he closed, "I may be seeing you very very soon. Goodnight, Beloved. It cannot be too soon."

Because he was assisting Mr. Winsbury White with a private case, he had to be up and out early next morning.

In a few minutes I must sally forth into a wet cold day. I am wondering what you have up your sleeve to say "Come at once." You see if I am to have no job I would as soon stay on in one until the middle of December, for being unable to practice & no job will not be fun. Of course there will be plenty of studying to do. Darling, I must away.

As we grew up, my sister Margaret and I knew that our mother could be forceful—fair but forceful. She used to tell of a Quaker adviser at Swarthmore College in Pennsylvania dissuading her from a nursing career: "I think, Dorothy, thee would do better giving orders than taking them." John was about to experience the wisdom of that advice.

"My Darling, things do move rapidly. I have received your telegram. It is certainly to the point. What lots I will have to do in the 6 days at my disposal." Although her telegram has not survived, Dorothy must have looked up the schedule of sailings from Southampton and suggested firmly to John that he be aboard the Cunard Line's *Berengaria*, departing for New York on November 22. He seemed chastened.

Darling, do you realize that within two weeks I will be with you. I must admit that I am a little scared of all that lies ahead of me. After the carefree irresponsible existence I have led for the past few years to take on the responsibilities I have assumed & from a wandering nomad to suddenly change to a settled citizen are both steps that give one much to think about. You will have to be patient & let me down lightly. You have been a member of a settled community all your life. Darling, I need you with me now to assure me that you will not become insular & that you will not expect me to apply for the post of mayor or even town councillor until I feel so disposed. You will not be perturbed if I do not reach that stage, will you, Darling? Dearest One, you have so much understanding to do. I am so very ordinary & know so very little. Still I will be with you soon, Wife of Mine, & come what may I'll do my darndest & grin the while. Goodnight, Wife of Mine. I do feel shy not of you as my sweetheart wife but as the established doctor. Darling, as I go off to sleep it is my wife I will think about. I do love her so.

Actually, he was relieved. "I am about to begin a busy day but I will have to forget about sleep for the next week. I can make up for any loss on the boat. Just think of it, within two weeks I will be with you. Have you any job in the offing? I hope so for I will want something to do." He had resigned his post at St. Paul's, although he remained on staff as long as he could. "I wrote a number of letters telling people I will be running off. To fit things in will be difficult. Still the main thing is to be on the boat when she sails." It was Thursday, November 16, twelve weeks since the Burnham Lodge Hotel. "Darling, tonight is 'our night.' I would that you were with me now. Believe me, I would not be writing any letter."

Although he complained of packing and of all the belongings he had accumulated, John managed during that last week to keep up his London routine. "A dull dark wet winter morning it is & I needs must go out for I am to see a chap's surgery this morning & get a few tips from him." Later that Friday, he told her,

Have had another interesting evening. Ended up by visiting Smoky Joe's, a low dive where lesbians & homosexuals frequent. It was interesting to sit & watch them. It gave one cause for much thought. Went to see "the [A] Sleeping Clergyman" with Atkins, a man from Park Prewett Hospital. It was an excellent play written on the subject of heredity by a doctor & against the idea. Have had a very busy day running around. Have definitely booked my berth on the *Berengaria*.

He seemed to relish the exhilaration of getting everything done, ticking off his list one item after another. "Of course I am excited," he wrote on Saturday morning,

Who could help being so when they were due to board the *Berengeria* in four days time & then better still meet a wife in ten days & such a wife. For you know—I don't mind admitting it now that I will be with you soon—you are extra special & I am extra lucky. Darling, I am having days like our days just before the wedding. But it is great fun rushing around trying to fit things in, knowing there are jobs to be done & places to be at certain times & all within a short, short time. Darling, I must away. The thought has just struck me that I will be bringing my next letter to you.

He did a round of the wards that morning, but packing hung over him "like a nightmare." Once it was done, he would breathe easier.

The amount of stuff I have accumulated is amazing, the quantity I am leaving is large & that to come along no mean order. My wardrobe arrived last morning. My suits really are well tailored & my heavy overcoat something to be proud of. I have enough suits to last me five years or so I hope. It was sad signing the cheque yet I feel it was a good investment. Darling, I will talk to you later in between packing & seeing people. My love to you, Sweetheart mine, John.

There were, of course, last-minute social obligations. "This evening I had Eleanor & Horace as visitors. I had a charming evening. I took them to a Japanese restaurant & had sukiyaki. They enjoyed cooking it & were quite good with chopsticks. Then we came back here. Horace was much impressed with your photos as well he might be."

John enclosed in his letter to Dorothy the note he received from them. They were so pleased he had devoted the entire evening to them.

> Here are our best wishes for a bon voyage—hope the fog lifts from the Channel and that you get all your packing done in good order. Don't forget us entirely. Our very best respects and good wishes to your lady Wife and also to you, old boy. Good cheer and God Speed in the new life you are commencing. Yours very sincerely, Eleanor H.

He had a long telephone conversation with Norah Marsh, "by no means well yet. I am to meet her tomorrow & have dinner with her on Tuesday," his last day before sailing. John said nothing about his goodbyes to Gwennie Oats.

In a P.S. to his Monday morning letter, he commented about a mutual acquaintance of theirs: "I was interested to learn of your meeting with Alec. It is sad to find him so unhappy, for marriage under those circumstances must be ghastly. We have made a splendid beginning, Maid of My Heart, & it is up to us to continue to have the grandest time." And that night, "Dorothy Darling, It is nearly 5 a.m. so I will say goodnight. Again have I had it exemplified that we are of the fortunates of this world. I will tell you about things in a few days. Packing etc. is just the very devil."

The last of nearly two hundred letters he had written to his wife in absentia over the past three months was barely a note, scribbled on Tuesday morning, November 21:

> Very, very soon after I climbed into bed I crawled out again. I have a fair few things to do so must away & at them. Me thinks

the hospital will see me but little. I lunch with Aubrey & dine with Norah. Life is grand but very, very, very full. Darling, I will be with you so very, very soon now & then, Beloved. Till then I send my love to you. Your loving husband, John.

In a subsequent letter to Cousin Bettina, written from Chalfonte-Hadden Hall, Atlantic City, N.J., on December 2, 1933, he described his hasty departure from London.

Believe me, I did get a hustle on to catch my ship. I had only six days to fix things up & I was working at the same time. By the aid of a couple of nights with only two hours sleep & the help of the Cockney night porter I was aboard the *Berengaria* when she sailed. There were such a number of large ships in Southampton, the *Aquitania*, the *Majestic*, the *Olympic*, the *Empress of Britain*, & the *Homeric*. Among all those goliaths was the *Moreton Bay* leaving the same day for Australia. We could have hoisted her on deck & used her for a lifeboat.

John delighted in his Atlantic crossing on the recently overhauled, 52,000-ton pride of the Cunard fleet with its updated interior.

We had a splendid trip with a gale for only one day. I had a large four berth cabin to myself. You should see the magnificent Pompeian swimming pool. We were allowed in each morning. The pitching of the ship made it more surfing than swimming. It was great exercise. It was wet on deck so that deck sports were off the list. We had a ping pong table. Good moving picture or dancing each evening. Some of the people were interesting & I had some excellent talks—a very cosmopolitan crowd.

Earlier from London, he had lovingly threatened Dorothy, "You wait until I have you in my arms; sailors, port officials, customs officers, none of them will be able to save you from the big kissing you are in for."

The *Berengaria* docked in New York on November 28, a Tuesday. As Dr. Lottridge, Dorothy enjoyed certain privileges.

Dorothy came aboard as a special reporter to interview me at the Quarantine Station. It was a grand interview we had but needless to say was not reported. A honeymoon taken on the instalment plan has much to recommend it. I see no reason why we can't go on indefinitely a few days at a time when opportunity offers. Bettina, I have the grandest of wives & this marriage business is great. Good luck to you, young lady. I hope Uncle & Auntie are keeping fit & well. With love to you all, John.

As he closed his letter to Bettina, he slipped into the envelope an undated note from Dorothy:

Dear Bettina, It was very charming of you to write as soon as you knew of our marriage, and I can't tell you how happy it made me. Having John here a month earlier than we had dared even hope is grand. There is much to be done at present. Finding an office which is suitable for him, fitting it out, having him meet the local doctors is keeping us much occupied at present. As soon as John arrived we went to Atlantic City to continue our painfully brief honeymoon. Leaving England two days after we were married was a ghastly business, believe me. But now that he is here all's right with my particular little world. Do save your pennies and come across to see us. John is so very fond of you that I'm especially anxious to actually have you visit us. For the present, letters will have to bridge the gap—but I do want to really know you. Affectionately, Dorothy.

A tiny notice that appeared in the *New York Herald-Tribune* for November 28, 1933, announced:

Another voyager on the Berengaria is Dr. John S. Kessell, Australian surgeon who has been practicing recently as a member of the staff of St. Paul's Hospital, in London. He recently married in London Dr. Dorothy Lottridge, of East Orange, N.J. He was unable to obtain leave and she returned here the day after their wedding to continue her practice as head of a special bureau of the Orange Memorial Hospital. Dr. Kessell arrives on a quota visa and will become an American citizen.

So ended John and Dorothy's three months of separation, and so began 30 years of utter devotion.

8

EPILOGUE: JOHN AND DOROTHY IN NEW JERSEY AND CALIFORNIA

The earliest personal prayer I ever remember saying, probably when I was about eight, presumptuous at any age, was simply, "Dear God, please don't take one without the other." In my mind, they were inseparable.

Dorothy and John lived for nearly a decade in East Orange with her parents, Silas A. and Alice D. Lottridge, in the large three-story house where she had her office. Her father, 70, was a retired high-school chemistry teacher; Thomas A. Edison, who located one of his workshops nearby in West Orange, once remarked that he would have no one else teach his son Theodore. Silas was also a tennis player, photographer, naturalist, and friend of John Burroughs. His only child, Dorothy, was born on February 18, 1900. One of his most beguiling photographs has three-year-old Dorothy in a white dress seated at Burroughs's knee on the top step of the latter's cabin "Slabsides." When her father's second book for Henry Holt and Company, *Familiar Wild Animals*, appeared in 1906, it was affectionately dedicated "To Dorothy Who Loves Animals."

Dorothy and John Burroughs, about 1903

From all indications, the Lottridges accepted their Australian son-in-law in the loving manner he had hoped for. The dreaded board exams required before Dr. Kessell could practice medicine and surgery in New Jersey proved not so great an obstacle. He presented sufficient evidence to the University of the State of New York to be granted license no. 28764, dated February 1, 1934, evidently without further exams. The original of his transcript at the University of Adelaide still has his New Jersey address penciled in the upper right-hand corner. He had received his Bachelor of Medicine, Bachelor of Surgery (the equivalent of an M.D.) in 1923, subsequently serving as Resident Medical Officer at Adelaide Hospital in 1924 and then at Broken Hill and District Hospital in 1925 and 1926, where he met Gwennie Oats. From 1927 until 1930, the young doctor practiced in Adelaide. In 1929, the University appointed him honorary demonstrator, or teaching assistant, in Anatomy, a position he resigned on May 14, 1930, "owing to my departure abroad almost immediately."

Having convinced the State of New York, Dr. Kessell had no trouble with New Jersey, which awarded him a license on April 24, 1934. Certification by the National Board of Medical Examiners followed on January 17, 1935, proclaiming that John Samuel Kessell had satisfied all the requirements and "successfully passed the examinations." He and Dorothy sent out a card announcing that he was opening an office at 643 Central Avenue, East Orange, for the practice of urology.

Dr. Dorothy Lottridge, having studied at Swarthmore College, Cornell University, and Women's Medical College, had received her M.D. in 1926. After their marriage, she continued practicing general medicine out of the family home. For the two doctors, the remainder of the 1930s proved eventful. I was born in 1936, Margaret Ann in 1938; our father became a naturalized U. S. citizen in 1939 (5' 6½" tall, 162 lbs., and no visible distinctive marks); Grandfather Lottridge died early in 1940; and Grandfather Kessell died in Australia the following year.

John's Certificate of U.S. Citizenship

John and Dorothy, right from the start, did almost everything together, not because they thought they should but simply because they loved each other's company. When the Nutley Badminton Club challenged the Grace Court Club of Brooklyn in April 1934, they entered as a mixed doubles team. In July of the same year, at Camp of the Woods in the Adirondacks, they hiked, swam, and canoed. "Paddling is quite an art," they wrote in a photo album prepared for her father. "The one in the stern does the steering with the paddle always on the same side." They attended the American Medical Association meetings at Atlantic City together a year later and again in 1937. About the latter, John wrote in a scrapbook, "The meetings and scientific exhibits were good but the ocean and the boardwalk were better."

Canoeing, Camp of the Woods, New York, 1934

John and Dorothy, A.M.A. Convention, Atlantic City, 1935

Eight weeks after my birth in April 1936, Dorothy wrote to Cousin Bettina in Australia, "John & I had our first tennis of the season this morning. It did seem so good to be able to take some really active exercise again." (Margaret and I remember that, even when we were teenagers, our parents could always beat us and our friends at ping pong.) An especially happy vacation for all four of us, judging by the snapshots our parents took, came in July 1940 when the family sailed aboard the steamer S.S. *St. John* from New York City to Portland, Maine, then drove to Deer Isle for two weeks in a cottage half in the woods and half on the shore

The satisfying, interwoven lives of the two doctors and their children came apart soon after the surprise attack on Pearl Harbor on December 7, 1941, as did the lives of most American families. At that moment, our father's taste for Japanese color prints and sukiyaki seems to have vanished. As a native of a threatened country in the Pacific, Kessell wanted to serve in the U.S. Navy. But the Navy rejected him, citing an overbite, the result of having his front teeth knocked out playing varsity lacrosse during medical school. "But I'm not going to bite the Japs," he protested.

Disappointed, the 43-year-old Australian joined the U.S. Army Air Corps as a medical officer with the rank of captain. A card announced that he was closing his office on October 23, 1942; patients would have access to their records at the office of Dr. Lottridge. Entering on active duty October 29, Captain Kessell would serve three years, five months, and nine days. As the family saw him off from Newark for officer training school in Miami Beach, Florida, another long separation began for Dorothy and John.

John S. and John L. Kessell

Adelaide University Inter-Varsity Lacrosse Club
(J. S. Kessel[l] top row, third from right)

Dorothy did not fare well. Although she had help with her two young children, she suffered severe separation anxiety. Margaret and I were sent to live for a brief while with cousins Ray and Helen Willard of New Berlin in upstate New York, birthplace and burial place of our maternal grandfather. The Air Corps, meanwhile, assigned John to the base hospital at Hammer Field on the outskirts of Fresno in California's central San Joaquin Valley. There, on dry temperate days, amid vineyards and eucalyptus trees, it was as if he had been transported back to South Australia. Why not relocate the family to California, at least temporarily? Dorothy agreed.

Much restored and accompanied by her friend Helen Goodell (whose broken leg ten years earlier, in retrospect, seemed providential),

Dorothy drove her widowed mother to New Berlin, then set out on June 7, 1943, cross-country for three thousand miles, two women and two small children. It was her first trip west. Dorothy would never forget picnicking on a tiny green island of lawn in arid Utah or descending the hair-raising Kingsbury Grade to Lake Tahoe in mountains the likes of which she had never seen before. Temporarily settled in Fresno, with us two kids in school, Captain Kessell received orders transferring him to Tonopah Army Air Base in the desert desolation of Nevada. On a postcard of a coyote, he reported that "the planes fly all day long & most of the night here. There are a few B-17s & a few single engine planes here but most are B-24s." His duty required riding out in an ambulance at all hours to crash sites and caring for survivors.

Dr. Lottridge, meanwhile, took a job with the State of California Department of Health, first conducting well-baby clinics at migrant labor camps and elsewhere in the valley (which entitled her to extra gas and tires during the war), then as physician in charge of women's health at Fresno State College. Her husband, back again at Hammer Field, found himself in charge of a ward of wounded Japanese officers, POWs who in gratitude for his care presented him with a collection of exquisite silk military insignias.

On April 7, 1946, five days after my tenth birthday, Captain Kessell returned to civilian life, which meant starting a medical practice all over again. First, however, having decided to make the move west permanent, our parents drove the family all the way back to New Jersey to sell the East Orange house, settle their affairs, and put whatever they wished to keep in a moving van for California. "It was a hectic time," John wrote to Bettina and her husband Bob Gowing in Australia. "However we had a very enjoyable return trip across the country."

Soon thereafter, the family, accompanying Dr. Lottridge to meetings at the Asilomar Conference Center, discovered our favorite vacation destination, the Monterey Peninsula and nearby Carmel.

Almost every August, we rented a cottage in the pines just outside the gates of Asilomar in Pacific Grove for two weeks (which generally included their wedding anniversary), and again on Christmas afternoon we drove from Fresno over Pacheco Pass for three or four days there. Nothing delighted us more than searching for a couple of driftwood boards and a long tube of kelp to string between them as a net, drawing a court in the wet sand, and tossing a cloth-covered rope quoit in a game of "rings," our beach version of deck tennis.

John and Dorothy on Asilomar Beach, California, 1962

Meanwhile, our parents had bought a small second house in Fresno, downtown at 1543 O Street, and converted it into two doctors' offices. Each sent out cards. As part of their practice, quite naturally they became popular marriage counselors. A couple could see them for the required blood tests, our mother would meet with the bride-to-be and our father with the groom, then they would all get together. Their regular patients appreciated that they made house calls and accepted a lug of grapes or a dressed goose from those who could not pay.

At home, our mother was more often the disciplinarian, our father the reconciler. Although our family experienced the usual growing pains and tensions, Margaret and I remember a secure routine. Our doctor parents would be off on their rounds in the morning, lunch together at their dual office, see patients in the afternoon, break for tea about four o'clock, and return home about six to read the paper and sip a glass of sherry. Margaret and Mom put dinner on the table, Dad and I regularly did the dishes. On Wednesday afternoons, they gardened together.

When our father's physician noted his irregular heartbeat in January 1963, he asked that John enter the hospital for tests. His Congregational minister stopped in for a chat that greatly lifted his spirits. That evening, the last person to visit him reported that his eyes never shone brighter. He was to be released next day to resume limited medical practice. He died that night, January 24, of angina, at age 63. Dorothy put on a brave front but she simply willed not to live. Soon diagnosed with ovarian cancer, she died the following December.

My most enduring memory of our parents has them walking hand-in-hand along Asilomar Beach with our little black-and-white cocker spaniel Timmie at their heels. Never in my life since have I known a more loving or devoted couple. To have grown up an intimate part of such a family gives me cause to echo my father's frequent proclamation to Dorothy from London in 1933: "I am the luckiest of men." With an emphatic nudge from her, John had kept his promise. He made it to East Orange by Christmas.

www.ingramcontent.com/pod-product-compliance
Lightning Source LLC
Chambersburg PA
CBHW030527260626
47157CB00005B/1920